Soup
BIBLE

Soup

BIBLE

Contents

Introduction

It all began with a few bones and vegetables thrown into a primitive pot with some water and wild herbs. Soup evolved as a staple all over the world and local specialities developed as cooks used the ingredients that were available to them. While it is now truly international fare, soup remains true to its original form — simple to make and full of flavor.

The wonderful thing about soup is not just the wide range of flavors and textures that can be achieved. It is enormously versatile and can be a light lunch, a palate-pleasing starter, or a one-pot meal. And with shortcuts such as a good-quality bought stock, soup is a great fast food for busy people.

The Basics

Making soup is easy. But it helps to have some good basic equipment. A 4–5 quart heavy-based saucepan with a lid is indispensable for all soup recipes. You will also need a fine sieve through which to strain the liquid back into the saucepan for thin soups.

An electric blender, food processor, hand-held blender or food mill are also invaluable. The texture of a soup will vary according to which of these you use: a blender (or hand mixer) produces a smooth purée; a food processor or food mill, a coarser purée. A hand mixer is particularly convenient, as you can do all the work in the saucepan. It is always best to cool the soup a little first before blending. Make sure that you do not overfill the blender or food processor.

Storing soups

Soup is the perfect fare for busy cooks, because it stores well. Most vegetable-based soups will keep in the refrigerator for three to four days. Soups containing meat, seafood and poultry can be stored for two to three days. Keep the soup in an airtight container, or in a bowl covered with cling-wrap. Soups also freeze well.

Pantry standbys

With a few basics in your pantry or refrigerator, you can whip up a soup in no time at all when you bring home the fresh ingredients. A shortlist:

PANTRY

- olive oil
- good-quality bought stock (boxes, pouches)
- canned chickpeas and beans (e.g. cannellini)
- legumes, especially dried beans and lentils
- grains, especially rice, pearl barley and couscous

- mini toasts
- onions, garlic, potatoes
- dried herbs, especially bay leaves and thyme
- spices, from basics such as peppercorns (and celery seeds, which are a convenient substitute for fresh celery) to the special flavors of your preferred cuisines

REFRIGERATOR
- celery, parsley, carrots and fresh ginger
- (freezer) ravioli or other small filled pasta, especially cheese-filled

Special Ingredients
These ingredients were substituted with their US counter-parts throughout the text:

- Beetroot - Beet
- Capsicum - Pepper
- Celeriac — Celery Root
- Coriander - Cilantro
- Risoni - Orzo

Extra touches

You can turn plain soups into something special, with a simple garnish and or accompaniment. Here are a few suggestions.

CRUNCH APPEAL

Toasted pieces of bread add texture and contrast to purée soups.

Croutes are thin slices of bread (traditionally a French baguette, but you can use just about any European-style loaf) brushed with olive oil and baked in a preheated oven (350°F) for 8–10 minutes until crisp and brown. Rub garlic or other seasonings into the bread before or after baking, for more flavor.

Croutons are cubes of bread fried in oil until crisp and brown. Alternatively, you can bake them on a lightly oiled tray in a preheated oven (350°F) for 4–8 minutes or until well colored. For garlic croutons, rub with a clove of garlic right after cooking.

Pita toasts are also delicious. Cut oval pita bread into quarters, open up and separate into triangles. Lightly brush with oil and bake in a preheated oven (425°F) for 8–10 minutes until crisp and brown.

CREAMY ADDITIONS

Yogurt (plain), **buttermilk** and **sour cream** are excellent lower-fat substitutes for cream in soups. They may curdle if boiled, so are best stirred into the soup just before serving.

Crème fraîche is also an excellent garnish or thickener, and does not curdle when boiled or added to hot soups. You can make your own crème fraîche by combining 1 pint cream with ½ pint buttermilk in a saucepan and heating until just warm. Remove to a bowl. Cover with cling-wrap, leaving a small gap for air. Stand at room temperature overnight or until thickened. Chill until ready to use.

FRESH HERBS

Chopped or shredded herbs make a colorful, flavorful fresh garnish. Choose herbs that suit the origins of your soup, or its main ingredient. Cilantro leaves, Kaffir lime leaves, Asian mint, and basil are perfect for Asian-style soups. Basil also, of course, goes beautifully with tomatoes and other summer vegetables such as zucchini. Chervil loves cucumber, peas, potatoes and leeks, and is an elegant garnish for chilled soups. Parsley and chives are traditional favorites. In fact, the possibilities of fresh herbs are limitless — so experiment.

Stock

The most important basic ingredient for a delicious soup is a full-flavored stock. Stocks are easy to make and can simmer away at the back of the stove while you're doing other things. Stock will keep in the refrigerator for up to a week, and freezes well.

In many recipes one stock can be substituted for another; for example, a vegetable stock can be used instead of a meat-based one. A fish stock should, generally speaking, only be used for a fish soup, but sometimes chicken stock can be substituted.

While home-made stock is almost always best, especially for clear soups, the fact is that these days you can find very good-quality stocks in delis, markets and even supermarkets — usually in boxes or pouches. Cubes and powders are a useful standby, but give a less natural flavor. They can be quite salty, so be careful if adding salt to the soup.

Beef Stock

4½ pounds beef bones

2 onions, quartered

2 carrots, peeled and coarsely
    chopped

2 stalks celery, coarsely chopped

4 cloves garlic, crushed

4 quarts water

10 black peppercorns

4 sprigs parsley

4 bay leaves

Preheat oven to 425°F. Place beef bones in a shallow roasting pan and roast for 40 minutes, turning occasionally. Add vegetables and cook for 15–20 minutes. Remove from oven and, using a slotted spoon to drain off any excess fat, place bones and vegetables in a large saucepan.

Pour in water and add the herbs and spices. Bring to a boil and then simmer over a low heat for 4–5 hours, skimming the top from time to time. Remove from heat and then strain. Cool stock before refrigerating. When cold, remove any fat that has settled on the top. Freeze or use as required.

MAKES 3 QUARTS

Chicken Stock

2 pounds chicken bones, skin removed (include a few chicken feet)

4 stalks celery, roughly chopped

2 carrots, peeled and coarsely chopped

2 onions, coarsely chopped

1 leek, chopped

8 black peppercorns

1 sprig each fresh parsley and thyme

1 bay leaf

1 strip lemon zest

2 quarts water

Place all ingredients in a large saucepan, cover and bring to boil. Remove lid and simmer for about 1 hour, skimming the top with a spoon frequently to remove any scum. Check seasoning and continue cooking for an additional hour.

Remove from heat and strain. Cool before refrigerating. When cold, remove any fat that has settled on the top. Freeze or use as required.

MAKES 2 QUARTS

Fish Stock

2 pounds fish bones and heads

1 onion, sliced into rings

1 stalk celery, sliced

1 sprig each fresh parsley
    and thyme

2 bay leaves

1 star anise (optional)

6 black peppercorns

1 cup white wine

1 strip lemon zest

1⅓ quarts water

Wash the fish heads and bones under cold running water. Cut into 4–5 pieces. Place all ingredients in a large saucepan and slowly bring to a boil. Simmer for 20 minutes, skimming off any surface scum. Remove from heat and strain into a bowl, then cool and refrigerate. Freeze or use as required.

A quick fish stock can also be made from prawn, lobster or crab shells. Use the same ingredients as for fish stock, but use shells instead of fish bones.

MAKES 1 QUART

Vegetable Stock

2 large carrots, peeled and sliced

2 onions, quartered

2 leeks, sliced

1 stalk celery, chopped

1 tomato, halved

2 cloves garlic, peeled

2 sprigs fresh herbs
  (e.g. thyme, oregano)

1 bay leaf

6 peppercorns

1 tablespoon yeast extract
  (optional)

2 quarts water

Place all ingredients in a large saucepan and bring to a boil. Simmer, uncovered, for 45 minutes, then strain. Cool and refrigerate or freeze until ready to use.

MAKES 2 QUARTS

To Clarify Stock

Particularly for a clear soup, it's advisable to remove any fat and other impurities from the stock so that you end up with a crystal-clear liquid.

To clarify 1 quart of stock, you will need 2 egg whites and 1 crushed egg shell. Whisk the whites and add to the stock with the crushed shell. Bring stock to a very gentle simmer and leave for 20–30 minutes: the sediments will attach themselves to the egg whites and a thick scum will rise to the surface. Remove the pot from the heat and leave to stand for 15–20 minutes. Now simply push the scum aside and ladle the stock through a sieve lined with a damp cloth. Allow to cool, then refrigerate or freeze until needed.

Mainly Vegetables

While most soups contain veggies, in some they take center stage. There are hearty winter warmers chock-full of beans and root vegetables, ephemeral treats featuring seasonal veggies such as early spring asparagus or full-flavored tomatoes in summer, and velvety purée soups ranging in color from creamy white to orange, red and bright green.

The recipes that follow feature veggies above all, but of course you will find vegetable-based soups in most of the other sections too.

Vegetarians can just substitute vegetable stock where meat or chicken stock is specified in a recipe.

Hearty Vegetable Soup with Olive Crostini

SOUP

1 tablespoon olive oil

2 parsnips, peeled and cut into small chunks

1 leek, thinly sliced

2 stalks celery, thinly sliced

2 cloves garlic, crushed

4 cups chicken stock

4 potatoes, peeled and cut into small chunks

2 tablespoons tomato paste

7 ounces fresh broad beans, such as fava (or use frozen)

4 ounces dried angel's-hair pasta, broken into 4-inch pieces

½ cup black-olive tapenade

CROSTINI

4 slices ciabatta

2 tomatoes, finely chopped

In a large saucepan heat oil and cook parsnip, leek, celery and garlic over a gentle heat for 6–8 minutes, stirring occasionally. Add stock, potatoes and tomato paste and bring to a boil. Simmer gently for 30 minutes until potato is just tender.

Add beans and pasta. Cook for 10–15 minutes until pasta is tender. Stir in 2 tablespoons of the olive tapenade.

For the crostini, grill the ciabatta on both sides and spread remaining tapenade over. Top with the chopped tomatoes. Ladle soup into deep bowls and float crostini on top.

SERVES 4

Roasted Vegetable Soup with Lentils

2 tablespoons virgin olive oil

1 large eggplant, cut into small pieces

1 large red pepper, deseeded and cut into small pieces

1 green or yellow pepper, deseeded and cut into small pieces

1 red onion, roughly chopped

4 cloves garlic, crushed

4 cups vegetable stock

14 ounces canned tomatoes, roughly chopped

14 ounces canned brown lentils, drained

1 tablespoon ground cumin

salt and freshly ground black pepper

½ cup yogurt

Preheat oven to 425°F. Pour oil into a shallow baking pan and place in oven to heat. When hot, place eggplant, pepper, onion and garlic in baking pan and baste with oil. Roast for 20–30 minutes until lightly browned and tender.

Meanwhile, heat stock in a saucepan and add tomatoes, lentils and cumin. Remove cooked vegetables from oven and add to saucepan. Stir, and season to taste. Ladle soup into bowls and spoon in a little yogurt for garnish.

SERVES 4

Moroccan Lentil Soup with Harissa

1 tablespoon olive oil

2 large onions, finely chopped

2 medium carrots, peeled and
 finely chopped

3 cloves garlic, finely chopped

1 teaspoon sweet paprika

1 teaspoon ground cumin

3 cups chicken or vegetable stock

2 cups green lentils, rinsed
 and drained

½ teaspoon harissa (optional)

salt

¼ teaspoon freshly ground
 black pepper

2 tablespoons finely chopped
 fresh mint

1 tablespoon lemon juice

lemon wedges

Heat oil in a large saucepan and sauté onions, carrots and garlic with the spices. Cook for about 4–6 minutes until vegetables are soft. Add stock, lentils, harissa, salt and pepper and bring to a boil. Simmer, uncovered, for about 45 minutes until lentils are tender.

Remove from heat and stir in mint and lemon juice. Serve immediately with extra harissa to taste and a squeeze of lemon juice. >

You can buy ready-made harissa in delis and supermarkets. It's easy to make your own, though, and it will keep for several months in the refrigerator. In a blender, purée together 1 whole head garlic (skin removed), ½ pound fresh chilies, 3 tablespoons finely chopped fresh mint, 3 tablespoons finely chopped fresh cilantro, 1 tablespoon salt and 1–2 tablespoons olive oil. Add more oil if needed, to produce a chunky paste. Place any unused harissa in a sterilized jar, pour over a little oil to cover, then seal jar and refrigerate.

SERVES 4

Lentil and Tomato Soup with Feta Cheese

2 tablespoons olive oil

1 large onion, finely chopped

4 large tomatoes, roughly
    chopped

4 ounces brown lentils

2 cups tomato juice

3 cups vegetable stock

½ teaspoon dried thyme

salt and freshly ground
    black pepper

2 tablespoons roughly chopped
    feta cheese

In a saucepan heat oil and add onion. Cook over a gentle heat until soft.
Add tomatoes, lentils, tomato juice, stock and seasonings. Slowly bring
to a boil and then simmer, covered, for 30–40 minutes until lentils are
tender. Season to taste. Ladle into bowls and garnish with the feta cheese.

SERVES 4

Spiced Red Lentil Soup

1½ tablespoons butter

1 onion, finely chopped

3 cloves garlic, finely chopped

1 tablespoon finely grated
  fresh ginger

½ teaspoon chili flakes

½ teaspoon ground turmeric

½ teaspoon ground coriander

½ teaspoon ground cumin

2 carrots, peeled and chopped

2 cups canned tomatoes,
  roughly chopped

1 cup red lentils

3 cups vegetable stock

salt and freshly ground
  black pepper

¼ cup creamy yogurt

1 tablespoon finely chopped
  fresh mint

In a saucepan melt butter and add onion, garlic, ginger and spices. Cook over medium heat until onion is soft. Add carrots, tomatoes, lentils and stock. Slowly bring to a boil. Cover the pan and gently simmer for about 40 minutes or until lentils are tender. Season to taste. Ladle into soup bowls and spoon over a little yogurt and mint for garnish.

SERVES 4

Mexican Bean Soup
with Tomato Salsa

2 tablespoons olive oil

2 onions, finely chopped

3 cloves garlic, finely chopped

1 teaspoon ground cumin

1 teaspoon ground coriander

2 cups dried black beans
(or use red kidney beans)

6 cups water

3 tomatoes, chopped

1 teaspoon salt

salt and freshly ground pepper

1 red onion, finely chopped

½ pound cherry tomatoes,
roughly chopped

1 small red or green chili,
seeded and thinly sliced

6 sun-dried tomatoes, drained
and thinly sliced

½ teaspoon salt

2 tablespoons finely chopped
fresh cilantro

In a large saucepan, heat oil and add onions, garlic, cumin and coriander. Cook over a low heat until soft. Add beans and water. Slowly bring to a boil and cook for about 1 hour at a low simmer or until beans are tender.

When beans are cooked, stir in the tomatoes and salt. Remove from heat and cool a little.

Meanwhile, make the tomato salsa. Mix all ingredients together in a bowl, then set aside until ready to use. >

Place 2 cups of the soup in a blender or food processor and purée. Return to the pan, season to taste and gently heat soup through. To serve, ladle into soup bowls and spoon a little of the tomato salsa over.

SERVES 4–6

Tuscan Lentil Soup

½ pound brown lentils

1 onion, chopped

1 stalk celery, chopped

1 carrot, chopped

2 quarts chicken or vegetable
   stock

2 cloves garlic, finely chopped

6 anchovies, finely chopped

2 tablespoons chopped parsley

6 fresh sage leaves

4 ounces olive oil

12 peppercorns, roughly crushed

Put the lentils in a large pot with the onion, celery, carrot and stock, and simmer for about 1 hour or until tender. Towards the end of the cooking time, remove lid so that liquid reduces a little.

When vegetables are cooked, add garlic, anchovies, parsley, sage, oil and peppercorns. Stir to combine, then remove soup from heat and leave to stand for at least an hour. Reheat and serve.

SERVES 4–6

Chunky Root Vegetable Soup

1½ tablespoons butter

1 tablespoon olive oil

6 medium carrots, peeled and
cut into chunks

2 large onions, roughly chopped

2 large leeks, thinly sliced

2 turnips, peeled and cut into
small chunks

2 parsnips, peeled and cut into
small chunks

1 small sweet potato, peeled
and cut into small chunks

1 large potato, peeled and cut
into small chunks

6 cups chicken stock

½ cup cream

salt and freshly ground
black pepper

2 tablespoons chopped
fresh chives

In a saucepan melt butter with oil. Add carrots, onions, leeks, turnips and parsnips and cook, stirring occasionally, over gentle heat until lightly browned. Add sweet potato, potato and stock. Slowly bring to a boil and simmer, covered, for about 20 minutes or until vegetables are tender. Remove from heat and cool a little.

Place half the soup in a food processor and purée. Return to the saucepan and stir in cream. Gently reheat and season to taste. Ladle into bowls and garnish with chives.

SERVES 4–6

Sherried Mushroom Soup

2 tablespoons olive oil

1–2 cloves garlic, finely chopped

1 small carrot, finely chopped

½ teaspoon celery seeds

1 large onion, finely chopped

4 cups sliced fresh mushrooms

¼ cup all-purpose flour

4 cups chicken stock

salt and pepper

½ cup dry sherry

⅔ cup cream

chopped fresh parsley to garnish

Heat oil in large pan, add garlic, carrot, celery seeds and onion, and cook gently for 15–20 minutes or until golden.

Add the mushrooms and cook for another 2 minutes. Stir in the flour and cook for 1 minute.

Gradually stir in the stock, then season with salt and pepper to taste. Bring to boil, cover and simmer for about 10 minutes. Stir in the sherry and cream, and heat through gently. Serve immediately, garnished with parsley.

SERVES 4–6

Spinach and Lentil Soup with Sesame Seeds

1 cup brown lentils

4 cups chicken or vegetable stock

1 tablespoon sesame oil

1 large red onion, finely chopped

1 stalk celery, thinly sliced

1 small carrot, peeled and thinly sliced

2 cloves garlic, crushed

1 teaspoon grated fresh ginger

1 bunch spinach, washed, stalks removed and leaves roughly chopped

2 tablespoons soy sauce

salt and freshly ground black pepper

2 tablespoons sesame seeds, lightly toasted

Place lentils and stock in a saucepan and bring to a boil. Simmer, covered, for about 35–40 minutes until tender.

Meanwhile, heat oil in a saucepan and cook onion, celery, carrot, garlic and ginger over high heat until vegetables are lightly browned. Pour in lentils and stock and stir for 2–3 minutes. Add spinach and soy sauce, and season to taste. Stir over medium heat until spinach is wilted, about 1–2 minutes. Ladle into bowls and garnish with sesame seeds.

SERVES 4

Italian Bean and Tomato Soup

2/3 pound white or cranberry beans

1 clove garlic

1 tablespoon olive oil

1⅓ pounds ripe tomatoes, peeled,
  deseeded and chopped

extra ⅓ cup olive oil

2 ounces chopped bacon (optional)

toasted breadcrumbs

Cover beans with water and soak overnight. Drain, then cook in plenty of
water with the garlic and 1 tablespoon oil, until beans are tender. Drain,
reserving 4 cups of the cooking liquid.

Meanwhile, heat the extra oil in a pan and cook the chopped tomatoes
for about 10 minutes with the chopped bacon. Set aside when cooked.

To serve, place some toasted breadcrumbs in each bowl, then add ½ cup
of the reserved cooking liquid. Add a few tablespoons of the tomato sauce,
and pile some beans on top.

SERVES 4

Minestrone with Pesto

SOUP

1 onion, sliced

¼ cup olive oil

2 large tomatoes, peeled and chopped

1.5 quarts water or stock

2 potatoes, peeled and diced

2 leeks, finely sliced

2 carrots, peeled and diced

1 cup cooked cannellini or white navy beans

1 zucchini, diced

9 ounces green beans, cut into 1¼-inch lengths

salt and freshly ground black pepper

freshly grated Parmesan cheese

PESTO

2 cloves garlic, chopped

1 cup loosely packed basil leaves

1 tablespoon finely chopped pine nuts

salt and freshly ground pepper

½–1 cup extra-virgin olive oil

In a large saucepan sauté the onion in the oil until softened. Add tomatoes and sauté for 5 minutes, then add water or stock and bring to a simmer. Add potatoes, leeks, carrots, and beans, and simmer for 45 minutes.

Add zucchini and green beans, and simmer for a further 15 minutes. Taste for seasoning. >

Meanwhile, make the pesto. Crush garlic and basil to a paste, using a mortar and pestle. Add the pine nuts, salt and pepper, and work into the basil mixture. Add the oil, little by little, stirring until well combined. (You can make the pesto in a blender, in which case process everything together, still adding the oil a little at a time.)

Just before serving, stir a tablespoon or two of the pesto into the soup. Ladle soup into bowls and offer Parmesan and remaining pesto on the side.

SERVES 4–6

Springtime Asparagus Soup

1⅔ pounds fresh asparagus, tough ends snapped off

2 tablespoons butter

1 large sprig fresh thyme

1 leek, sliced

2 cloves garlic, sliced

2 potatoes, peeled and chopped

1 quart chicken or vegetable stock

salt and freshly ground pepper

cream and extra chopped fresh thyme, to serve

Chop the asparagus, reserving 12 tips. Cook the tips in boiling salted water until tender, then drain and set aside.

Melt butter in a large saucepan and toss in the thyme, leek, garlic and potatoes for a few minutes. Add stock, then cover and simmer for 15 minutes until vegetables are quite tender. Now add the chopped asparagus and simmer for 5–10 minutes.

Blend the contents of the saucepan, and taste for seasoning. If there are any asparagus fibers evident, strain the soup through a fine sieve. Serve topped with a swirl of cream, the cooked tips (first warmed in a little butter) and the extra chopped thyme.

SERVES 4–6

Roasted Tomato and Pepper Soup

2¼ pounds ripe, firm (unpeeled) tomatoes, quartered, cored and deseeded

2 red peppers, cut into eighths, cored and deseeded

1 red onion, peeled and quartered

3 cloves garlic, unpeeled

a few sprigs fresh basil

4 tablespoons extra-virgin olive oil

4–6 cups chicken or vegetable stock

2 teaspoons balsamic vinegar

salt and freshly ground black pepper

extra chopped basil, to garnish

crusty bread, to serve

Preheat oven to 375°F.

Mix the peppers and tomatoes in a baking pan with the onion, garlic, basil and oil. Season with salt and pepper, then roast for 1 hour or until the edges of the tomatoes are slightly blackened.

When the vegetables are ready, remove from the oven. Remove the garlic cloves, squeeze out the pulp and discard the skins. Blend the contents of the baking pan (including all the juices) with the stock – leave the purée a little on the chunky side. Add balsamic vinegar to taste, and season with salt and pepper. >

Transfer soup to a pot and reheat gently. Serve in warmed bowls, topped with a little basil and accompanied by good crusty bread.

SERVES 4–6

🥣 For a special occasion, use fish stock and add 8–12 prawns to the soup when reheating.

Egyptian Vegetable Soup with Lemon and Mint

2 quarts chicken or vegetable stock

3 leeks, sliced thickly

1 head of celery (including leaves), sliced thickly

4 potatoes, peeled and diced

salt and pepper

4 cloves garlic, chopped

juice of 2 lemons, or to taste

1 teaspoon sugar, or to taste

4 zucchini, sliced

¼ cup chopped fresh mint

mint springs

Bring the stock to a boil in a large pot. Add the remaining ingredients, except the zucchini and mint, and simmer for about 30 minutes or until vegetables are tender.

Now add the zucchini and mint, and simmer for another 15 minutes or so until zucchini are cooked.

Serve in heated bowls, garnished with a sprig of mint.

SERVES 6

Golden Yogurt Soup with Rice and Chickpeas

⅓ cup rice

1¼ quarts chicken or vegetable stock

2 cloves garlic, crushed

pinch (4–6) saffron threads

pinch of ground turmeric

2 cups plain yogurt

2 tablespoons all-purpose flour

2 egg yolks

salt and pepper

14 ounces canned chickpeas, drained

fresh cilantro sprigs, to serve (optional)

Cook the rice in boiling salted water until tender, then drain.

Bring the stock to the boil in a large saucepan. Add the garlic, saffron threads and turmeric, and allow to infuse.

Beat the yogurt, flour and egg yolks in a bowl until combined, then season with salt and pepper to taste. Add this mixture to the stock, stirring as you do so, and continue to stir over a gentle heat until the soup begins to thicken. Add the rice and chickpeas, and heat through again. Serve in heated bowls, with a sprig of cilantro if you like.

SERVES 6

Pumpkin Soup with Cumin

3 tablespoons olive oil

2 onions, peeled and sliced

3⅓ pounds pumpkin, peeled and cubed

1 teaspoon salt

freshly ground black pepper

1 teaspoon ground cumin

3 sprigs of fresh thyme

4 cups chicken or vegetable stock

croutons (see page 4), to serve

Heat the oil in a heavy-based pot and add the onions. Sauté gently for
15 minutes until onions are soft.

Add the pumpkin to the pot. Sprinkle with salt, pepper, cumin and thyme,
cover, and sauté for another 15 minutes (check occasionally to make sure
that the vegetables do not burn).

Add the stock, cover, and then simmer for 30 minutes, until the pumpkin
is tender.

Blend the soup until smooth, then reheat. Check seasoning, and add more
salt and cumin if required.

SERVES 4–6

Kidney Bean and Spinach Soup

1 tablespoon olive oil

1 onion, finely chopped

2 cloves garlic, crushed

1 carrot, peeled and finely
chopped

1 stalk celery, finely chopped

1 corn cob, kernels stripped off

2 cups kidney beans, soaked
overnight

4 cups beef stock

1 bunch spinach, washed, stems
removed and leaves shredded

½ pound sliced pancetta
(optional)

In a large saucepan heat oil and gently cook onion, garlic, carrot and celery
for 4–5 minutes, stirring occasionally. Add corn kernels, drained kidney
beans, and stock. Bring to a boil and simmer, covered, for 30 minutes
or until beans are tender.

Meanwhile, grill or gently fry pancetta until crisp. When beans are cooked,
stir in spinach. Serve soup in deep bowls with crisped pancetta scattered
over the top.

SERVES 4

Garden Pea and Lettuce Soup

1 small butter lettuce

1 cup fresh mint leaves

1½ tablespoons butter

½ bunch spring onions, finely chopped

1 teaspoon sugar

1⅔ pounds fresh peas, shelled (or 1 pound frozen)

4 cups chicken stock

¼ cup cream

salt and freshly ground black pepper

Rinse and finely shred lettuce, reserving 4 leaves for garnish. Shred mint, reserving 6 leaves for garnish.

In a saucepan melt butter and add spring onions. Cook over a gentle heat until soft, then stir in sugar. Add peas and stock and slowly bring to a boil. Simmer, covered, for 15–20 minutes until peas are tender. Add shredded lettuce and mint leaves and cook an additional 2-3 minutes. Remove and cool a little.

Blend soup until smooth. Reheat, then stir in cream and season to taste. Ladle soup into bowls and garnish with reserved lettuce and mint. (This soup is also delicious served chilled.)

SERVES 4–6

Soup of Roasted Summer Vegetables

7 ounces tomatoes

1 onion, roughly chopped

3 young carrots, sliced lengthways into sticks

1 small bulb fennel, halved and sliced

2 large cloves garlic, sliced

3 tablespoons olive oil

1 medium zucchini, thickly sliced

1½ quarts vegetable stock

salt and freshly ground black pepper

2 bay leaves

4 ounces small pasta shapes

1 small cabbage heart (center leaves), shredded

1 cup torn fresh basil leaves

1-2 tablespoons grated Parmesan

extra-virgin olive oil, to serve

Preheat oven to 425°F. Put the tomatoes, onion, carrots, and fennel in a roasting pan. Add the garlic, then toss everything together with the olive oil. Roast for about 45 minutes, until the vegetables are soft and golden.

Put the roasted vegetables into a deep saucepan, add the zucchini and pour the stock over. Season with salt, pepper and bay leaves. Bring to a boil, then simmer for about 20 minutes.

Meanwhile, cook the pasta in boiling salted water until nearly tender (around 10 minutes). Drain. >

Stir the cooked pasta, the cabbage and half the basil into the soup and continue to simmer for 5 minutes or so.

Ladle into warm bowls, spoon over a little extra-virgin olive oil, then scatter with the remaining basil and the Parmesan.

SERVES 4–6

Cauliflower and Pistachio Soup

2 tablespoons olive oil

1 onion, finely chopped

2 cloves garlic, finely chopped

½ cauliflower, broken into
    florets

4 cups chicken stock

2 ounces shelled pistachio nuts

salt and freshly ground
    black pepper

freshly chopped chives

In a saucepan heat oil and add onion and garlic. Cook over medium heat until soft. Add cauliflower and stock and bring to a boil. Simmer for 15–20 minutes until cauliflower is tender. Remove and cool a little.

Place 3 cups of the soup in a food processor or blender with the pistachio nuts, and purée. Return to the saucepan. Season to taste. Serve immediately, garnished with chives.

SERVES 4

Spicy Broccoli Soup

1 tablespoon olive oil

1 large onion, roughly chopped

1 clove garlic, crushed

1 tablespoon ground coriander

1 teaspoon ground cumin

½ teaspoon ground turmeric

3 cups vegetable stock

1 cup coconut milk

2 pounds broccoli, broken into small florets

2 tablespoons chopped fresh cilantro

2 tablespoons mango chutney (optional)

4 cooked pappadums (Indian flatbreads)

In a large saucepan heat oil and cook onion and garlic gently for 4–5 minutes until onion is soft. Add ground spices and cook for 2–3 minutes. Pour in stock and coconut milk, and slowly bring to a boil. Add broccoli, reduce heat and simmer for 10–15 minutes. Remove from heat and cool a little.

Purée half the soup, return to the saucepan and reheat. Stir in chopped cilantro. Ladle soup into bowls and garnish with a dollop of chutney (if used) and cracked pappadums.

SERVES 4

Parsley Soup

1 large bunch flat-leaf parsley
1 leek (white and pale green parts
   only), chopped
2-3 tablespoons olive oil
2 small zucchini, cubed
½ teaspoon salt
¼ cup white wine
4 cups water or chicken stock
salt and freshly ground pepper

Separate parsley leaves from the stems, and chop stems coarsely.

Cook parsley stems and leek in oil in a heavy saucepan over low heat until softened, about 5 minutes. Add zucchini and salt, and cook, stirring, for 1 minute. Add wine and water or stock, then simmer, covered, until zucchini is very tender, about 10 minutes.

Add parsley leaves to the soup and purée mixture until smooth. Season with salt and pepper, before reheating.

SERVES 4

Classic French Onion Soup

2 tablespoons butter

4 large red onions, thinly sliced

1 teaspoon sugar

1 tablespoon balsamic vinegar

4 cups beef stock

1 cup red wine

salt and freshly ground black pepper

1 small French baguette, sliced into rounds

½ cup coarsely grated Swiss cheese

In a saucepan slowly melt butter and add onions. Cook over very low heat, stirring occasionally, for about 30 minutes until onion is soft and lightly browned.

Stir in sugar and balsamic vinegar. Cook an additional 5 minutes, then add stock and slowly bring to a boil. Add red wine and simmer, uncovered, for 15 minutes. Season to taste.

Meanwhile, toast bread rounds, spread with a little butter and top with the cheese. Ladle the soup into bowls, with the cheesy toasts floated on top.

SERVES 4–6

Mushroom Soup with Pearl Barley

1½ tablespoons butter

1 onion, finely chopped

2 cloves garlic, finely chopped

2 stalks celery, finely chopped

1 pound mushrooms, roughly chopped

¼ cup pearl barley

5 cups chicken stock

1 potato, peeled and roughly grated

¼ cup finely chopped fresh parsley, plus extra for garnish

salt and freshly ground black pepper

In a saucepan melt butter and add onion, garlic, celery, mushrooms and barley. Cook over a low heat for 20 minutes until mushrooms are soft. Add stock and potato, and bring to a boil. Simmer, covered, for 40 minutes until barley is tender and soup has thickened.

Stir in chopped parsley, and season to taste. Ladle soup into bowls and garnish with extra chopped parsley.

SERVES 4–6

Fava Bean and Olive Soup with Aioli

SOUP

1 cup fava beans (dried broad beans), soaked and drained

1 medium-sized potato, peeled and diced

1 leek, thinly sliced

1 cup pitted black olives

1 red onion, chopped

2 cloves garlic, finely chopped

2 sprigs fresh thyme

4 cups vegetable or chicken stock

salt and ground black pepper

AIOLI (GARLIC MAYONNAISE)

2 cloves garlic

salt

2 egg yolks

1–1½ cups olive oil

a little lemon juice

To make the soup, put everything in a large pot and bring gently to a boil. Cover, and simmer for 1 hour, or until beans are tender. Blend to a coarse purée (sieve before serving, to remove fibrous bean skins), and return to pot to reheat.

To make the aioli, crush the garlic with a little salt, using a pestle and mortar, then add the egg yolks and combine. Add the oil very gradually, whisking all the time, until thickened. Add lemon juice to taste.

Just before serving, stir in 2–3 tablespoons of aioli into the soup. Serve with toasted rustic-style bread on the side.

SERVES 4–6

Vietnamese-style Curry Soup

2 tablespoons vegetable oil

1 onion, coarsely chopped

2 spring onions, thinly sliced

2 cloves garlic, chopped

1 tablespoon thinly sliced fresh ginger

1 stalk lemongrass, cut into 1½-inch pieces

3 tablespoons Vietnamese or Madras curry powder

1 green pepper, deseeded, pith removed and flesh coarsely chopped

2 carrots, sliced diagonally

8 mushrooms, sliced

¾ pound fried tofu, cut into bite-sized pieces

1 quart vegetable stock

2 tablespoons vegetarian fish sauce (optional)

1 teaspoon chili flakes

1 bay leaf

2 kaffir lime leaves

8 small potatoes, quartered

14 ounces canned coconut milk

2 cups fresh bean sprouts, for garnish

8 sprigs chopped fresh cilantro leaves, for garnish

Heat oil in a large pot and sauté onion and spring onions until soft and translucent. Stir in garlic, ginger, lemongrass and curry powder. Cook for about 5 minutes, to release the curry flavors.

Add pepper, carrots, mushrooms, tofu and stock. Season with optional fish sauce and chili flakes. Bring to a boil, then stir in potatoes and coconut milk. Reduce heat and simmer for 20–30 minutes, or until potatoes are tender.

Serve in heated bowls, topped with bean sprouts and garnished with chopped cilantro.

SERVES 4–6

Mainly Fish

Just about every coastal community has its own fish soups, many of which evolved over centuries. Some are chunky, colorful stews, such as the bouillabaisse of the Mediterranean and the chowders popularized along the Atlantic seaboard, which make great one-pot meals. Bisques are rich, creamy concoctions traditionally based on shellfish. Asian cuisines have all sorts of fish soups, from delicate broths to spicy infusions.

As with any recipes containing fish, you should always buy the freshest fish possible. Fish cooks quickly, so needs to be added to the soup towards the very end: a chunk of white fish will take less than 10 minutes, while shellfish such as mussels, prawns and scallops need 3–4 minutes only. Suitable firm-fleshed fish for soups include snapper, catfish, haddock, sea bass, orange roughy and cod.

Catalan Fish Soup with Potatoes

1 tablespoon olive oil

1 large onion, finely chopped

3 cloves garlic, crushed

2 stalks celery, finely chopped

1 tablespoon ground paprika

1 teaspoon ground cumin

3 cups fish stock

pinch of saffron threads

1 cup white wine

2 bay leaves

14 ounces canned tomatoes, chopped

¾ pound potatoes, peeled and cut into small chunks

8 prawns, peeled and deveined

½ pound firm white fish fillets, cut into chunks

8 black mussels, cleaned and debearded

salt and freshly ground pepper

2 tablespoons finely chopped fresh parsley

In a large saucepan heat oil and gently cook onion, garlic, celery, paprika and cumin for about 4–5 minutes, stirring occasionally. Pour in stock, saffron, wine and bay leaves and bring to a boil. Add potatoes and tomatoes and simmer for 20 minutes until potatoes are tender. Remove from heat.

Blend one-third of soup to a purée. Return to the saucepan, add prawns and fish and cook for 2–3 minutes. Add mussels and cook for 2–3 minutes until shells open. Ladle into bowls and garnish with parsley.

SERVES 4

Spicy Coconut Fish Soup with Rice

1 tablespoon Thai green curry
  paste

1 carrot, peeled and roughly
  chopped

1 red onion, finely diced

1 stick lemongrass, finely
  chopped

⅓ pound pumpkin, peeled and
  roughly chopped

1½ cups vegetable stock

1½ cups coconut milk

1 cup jasmine rice

1 zucchini, roughly chopped

½ pound firm fish fillets, cut
  into small pieces

salt and freshly ground
  black pepper

3 tablespoons chopped fresh
  cilantro

coconut cream, to serve

In a large saucepan, sauté the curry paste with the carrot, onion,
lemongrass and pumpkin over a gentle heat for 2–3 minutes. Pour in stock
and coconut milk, and slowly bring to a boil. Add rice and simmer for
15–20 minutes until tender.

Add zucchini and fish. Cook for 4–5 minutes until fish is cooked. Season
to taste and stir in 2 tablespoons of the chopped cilantro. Ladle soup into
bowls and garnish with remaining cilantro and a little coconut cream.

SERVES 4–6

Fish Chowder

4 ounces bacon, roughly
    chopped

1 teaspoon olive oil

2 stalks celery, finely chopped

1 onion, finely chopped

4 cloves garlic, finely chopped

2 tablespoons tomato paste

28 ounces canned tomatoes,
    drained and roughly chopped

2 cups fish stock

1 cup white wine

2 bay leaves

1 medium-sized potato, peeled
    and cut into chunks

salt and freshly ground
    black pepper

3/4 pound firm fish fillets,
    cut into pieces

16 mussels, scrubbed and
    debearded

2 tablespoons finely chopped
    fresh parsley

In a saucepan fry the bacon in the oil for 2–3 minutes. Add celery, onion, garlic and tomato paste, and cook, stirring occasionally, for 6–7 minutes. Add tomatoes, stock, wine and bay leaves. Bring to a boil, add potato, season well and then simmer for 10–15 minutes until potato is just tender.

Add fish and poach for 3–4 minutes. Stir in mussels and cook for 2–3 minutes until they open. Check seasoning. Ladle into bowls and garnish with the chopped parsley.

SERVES 4

Bouillabaisse with Rouille

2 tablespoons olive oil

2 leeks, finely chopped

1 carrot, peeled and chopped

4 cloves garlic, finely chopped

1 bulb fennel, finely chopped

14 ounces canned tomatoes, drained and chopped

good pinch saffron threads

6 cups fish stock

1 teaspoon grated orange zest

salt and freshly ground black pepper

2 pounds mixed fresh seafood (fish fillets, prawns, mussels and/or clams)

chopped fresh parsley, to serve

ROUILLE

1 thick slice ciabatta or sourdough bread, crusts removed

2 cloves garlic, finely chopped

$\frac{1}{2}$ red pepper, cored and deseeded

$\frac{1}{2}$–1 teaspoon ground Spanish-style paprika

6 tablespoons olive oil

salt and freshly ground black pepper

To make bouillabaisse, heat oil in a large saucepan and add leeks, carrot, garlic and fennel. Cook, stirring over a gentle heat, for 8–10 minutes until soft. Stir in tomatoes, saffron, stock and orange zest. Bring to a boil and simmer for 30 minutes until liquid has reduced a little. Season to taste. >

Meanwhile, make the rouille. Soak bread in cold water for 2–3 minutes, squeeze dry and place in blender with the garlic, pepper and paprika. Blend to a paste with a little of the oil, then gradually add the remaining oil until mixture thickens. Season to taste.

Add fish in order of cooking times – thickest pieces first (about 6 minutes), delicate fish, prawns and mussels last (about 4 minutes).

Ladle soup into bowls and garnish with a little of the rouille and some chopped parsley.

Suitable fish for this stew-like soup include snapper and cod, as well as more delicate varieties such as hake or sea bass.

SERVES 4–6

Prawn and Corn Chowder

1 tablespoon butter

1 leek, thinly sliced

1 large sweet potato, peeled and
cut into small chunks

kernels from 3 corn cobs

4 ounces white wine

4 cups vegetable stock

salt and freshly ground
black pepper

4 ounces crème fraîche

7 ounces prawns, peeled
and deveined

1–2 tablespoons fresh lime juice

3 tablespoons roughly chopped
fresh cilantro

sprigs of fresh cilantro,
to serve

In a saucepan melt butter and add leek, sweet potato and corn kernels.
Cook over gentle heat for 5–8 minutes, stirring occasionally. Pour in stock
and season to taste. Bring to a boil and simmer for 15–20 minutes, until
vegetables are tender. Remove from heat and cool a little.

Purée half the soup in a blender. Return to the saucepan and stir in crème
fraîche and prawns. Gently reheat for 2–3 minutes, then stir in lime juice
and chopped cilantro. Ladle into bowls and garnish with cilantro sprigs.

SERVES 4

Thai Prawn and Pumpkin Soup

2 tablespoons fresh lime juice

2 pounds pumpkin, peeled and cut into small chunks

1 tablespoon olive oil

1 tablespoon Thai red curry paste

1 red onion, finely chopped

1 stick lemongrass, finely chopped

3 cups vegetable stock

12 prawns, peeled and deveined

1 cup coconut milk

1 tablespoon fish sauce

½ cup chopped fresh basil

Pour lime juice over pumpkin pieces and set aside. In a saucepan heat oil and add curry paste, onion and lemongrass. Cook over a gentle heat for 3–4 minutes. Pour in the stock, then add the pumpkin and lime juice. Slowly bring to a boil and simmer, covered, for 20 minutes until pumpkin is tender.

Add prawns and stir in coconut milk and fish sauce. Simmer for 2–3 minutes until prawns are cooked. Ladle soup into bowls, evenly distributing prawns, and garnish with the chopped basil.

SERVES 4

Cajun Prawn Gumbo

¼ cup olive oil

1 tablespoon all-purpose flour

4 cloves garlic, finely chopped

1 onion, finely chopped

2 stalks celery, finely chopped

1 red pepper, deseeded and finely chopped

1 green pepper, deseeded and finely chopped

6 spring onions, finely chopped

4 cups fish stock

28 ounces canned tomatoes, drained and chopped

2 bay leaves

1 teaspoon dried oregano

2 teaspoons dried thyme

1 teaspoon ground allspice

1 teaspoon ground sweet paprika

1 tablespoon filé powder (optional)

2 pounds prawns, peeled and deveined

salt and freshly ground black pepper

good dash of Tabasco sauce

juice of 1 lime

2 cups cooked rice

Heat the oil in a large saucepan and stir in flour. Cook, stirring, over a gentle heat for about 10–15 minutes, until flour is reddish-brown. Stir in garlic, onion, celery, peppers and spring onions, and cook over a low heat for 5–6 minutes. Slowly stir in stock and add tomato, herbs and spices. Bring to a boil, then simmer for 20 minutes.

Stir in prawns and poach for 3–4 minutes until cooked. Season to taste and add Tabasco sauce and lime juice.

To serve, spoon some rice into each bowl and ladle soup over.

Filé powder is a traditional Cajun thickener, made from dried and ground sassafras leaves. You can leave it out with no real effect on the flavor of the gumbo; some cooks use sliced fresh okra (1–2 cups), or even zucchini, instead.

SERVES 4 – 6

Moroccan Sweet Potato Soup with Fish Dumplings

SOUP

1 tablespoon butter

1 carrot, peeled and finely chopped

1 leek, finely chopped

1 clove garlic, crushed

2 teaspoons grated fresh ginger

1 teaspoon ground cumin

½ teaspoon ground turmeric

1 white sweet potato, peeled and chopped

4 cups vegetable stock

4 ounces spinach leaves, chopped

salt and ground black pepper

juice of 1 lime

chopped fresh chives

DUMPLINGS

½ pound rainbow trout or snapper, skin removed

1 tablespoon chopped fresh parsley

1 tablespoon chopped fresh chives

2 teaspoons grated fresh ginger

1 clove garlic, crushed

2 tablespoons lemon juice

1 teaspoon shredded lemon zest

Make the dumplings first. Blend all ingredients to a fine paste. Remove, then with wet hands shape into walnut-sized balls. Chill until ready to use.

To make soup, in a saucepan heat butter and add carrot, leek, garlic, ginger and spices. Cook for about 10 minutes over a gentle heat, stirring occasionally, until vegetables are soft. Add sweet potato and stock, and bring to a boil. Cover and simmer for 20 minutes until sweet potato is tender.

Add spinach and dumplings to the soup and cook for 2–3 minutes. Season to taste and stir in lime juice. Ladle soup into bowls and garnish with the chopped chives.

SERVES 4–6

Scallop and Artichoke Soup

2 pounds Jerusalem artichokes,
    scrubbed and thinly sliced

4 cups chicken or fish stock

pinch of ground nutmeg

salt and freshly ground
    black pepper

4 ounces crème fraîche or
    fresh cream

12 large fresh scallops

finely chopped chives

Place Jerusalem artichokes and stock in a large saucepan and slowly bring
to a boil. Simmer, covered, for about 30–40 minutes until artichokes are
tender. Remove from heat and cool a little, then blend until smooth.

Return soup to the saucepan and gently reheat. Add nutmeg and season
to taste. Stir in crème fraîche.

Just before serving, warm the soup bowls and put 3 scallops in each bowl.
Ladle in hot soup and garnish with chives. (The scallops will be cooked in
1–2 minutes.)

SERVES 4

Cullen Skink (a Scottish soup)

1–2 tablespoons butter

1 pound smoked-cod fillets

2½ cups milk

1 onion, finely chopped

4 potatoes, peeled and diced

2 quarts fish stock

2 bay leaves

salt and pepper to taste

7 ounces cream

chopped parsley, to garnish

strips of smoked salmon,
    to garnish (optional)

Grease a large pan with some of the butter, and add the cod (in one layer if possible). Pour the milk over, and gently bring to a simmer. Poach the cod until tender (about 10 minutes), then carefully remove (reserve the milk). Remove the cod when cool enough to handle, discard the skin and bones, and then flake the flesh and set aside.

In a large saucepan, melt the remaining butter and add the onion. Cook until soft and transparent, add the potatoes and continue cooking for 5 minutes. Add stock, bay leaves, salt and pepper. Simmer until the potato is tender, then strain in the reserved milk and add the flaked cod. Add the cream and reheat – the soup will be quite thick.

Serve in heated bowls, garnished with chopped parsley and, for a special touch, strips of smoked salmon.

SERVES 6

Creamy Fish Soup with Croutons

¼ cup olive oil

1 red onion, chopped

2 stalks celery, chopped

1 bulb fennel, chopped

2 cloves garlic, chopped

1 teaspoon finely sliced
orange zest

14 ounces can tomatoes

1 red pepper, deseeded and
sliced

1 bay leaf

1 sprig fresh thyme

4–6 saffron threads

1 pound fish fillets

6 prawns

1½ quarts fish stock

juice of 1 orange

salt and freshly ground pepper

good pinch of ground cayenne
pepper

garlic croutons, to serve
(see page 4)

Heat the oil in a large pan. Add the onion, celery, fennel and garlic,
and cook gently for about 15 minutes, until vegetables are soft but not
colored. Add orange zest, tomatoes, pepper, bay leaf, thyme, saffron and
fish fillets. Sauté, stirring, for 5 minutes, until fish begins to firm.
Add the prawns, stock and orange juice, and simmer for about 10 minutes.

Purée the soup in a blender, return to pan to reheat, and season with salt,
pepper and cayenne to taste. Serve with the croutons on the side.

SERVES 6

Mussel Soup with Garlic and Chili

4 ounces dry white wine

4 pounds mussels, scrubbed
and debearded

2 tablespoons extra-virgin
olive oil

4 cloves garlic, finely chopped

3 fresh small hot chilies (such as
Thai) deseeded and thinly
sliced

1 quart fish or chicken stock

1 cup fresh basil leaves

sea salt and freshly ground
pepper

crusty bread to serve (optional)

Place wine in a large heavy-based frying pan and bring to a boil. Add the mussels, in batches, and cook, covered, for 3 minutes or until shells open. Remove mussels with a slotted spoon and drain in a colander over a bowl. (Discard any mussels that have not opened.) Strain cooking liquid through a fine sieve, reserving ½ cup.

Heat olive oil in a saucepan, add garlic and two-thirds of the sliced chilies, and cook until garlic is golden-brown. Add stock and reserved mussel liquid, and simmer for 5 minutes. Add basil, and salt and pepper to taste.

Ladle mussels into warm bowls, then pour broth over and serve immediately with extra chili slices. Accompany with crusty bread if you like.

SERVES 4

Seafood Broth with Fish Dumplings

DUMPLINGS

⅔ pound snapper fillets

½ teaspoon each salt and freshly ground black pepper

1 spring onion, finely chopped

1 clove garlic, finely chopped

1 tablespoon finely chopped fresh parsley

1 teaspoon grated lemon zest

juice of 1 lemon

SOUP

4 cups fish stock

2 small carrots, cut into thin matchstick slices

1 large leek, cut into thin matchstick slices

1 small bulb fennel, chopped

2 star anise

½ teaspoon grated fresh ginger

½ cup dry white wine

2 spring onions, sliced thinly

To make dumplings, place everything except the lemon juice in a food processor and blend. Add juice and blend to a fine paste. With wet hands, roll mixture into walnut-sized balls. Chill until ready to use.

To make the broth, bring stock to a simmer. Add all the ingredients except the spring onions, and cook for 5 minutes. Remove star anise.

To assemble the soup, add dumplings to broth and cook for 2–3 minutes. Ladle soup into bowls and garnish with the sliced spring onions.

SERVES 4

Japanese Dashi Broth

4 ounces somen (wheat) or soba
(buckwheat) noodles

3 dried shiitake mushrooms

1½ quarts dashi

4 tablespoons mirin
(sweet rice wine)

2 tablespoons soy sauce

zest of 1 lemon, cut into strips

Cook noodles in boiling water, uncovered, until just tender. Drain.

Meanwhile, place mushrooms in small bowl, cover with boiling water
and leave until tender. Drain, and slice thinly.

Place remaining ingredients (except the lemon zest) in a large saucepan,
bring to a boil and simmer, uncovered, for 10 minutes.

Just before serving, divide noodles, mushrooms and lemon zest between
heated serving bowls. Ladle hot broth into bowls, and serve at once.

Dashi is a fish stock available as a liquid, powder or granules.
You'll find it in Asian food stores and some supermarkets.

SERVES 6

Asian Fish and Vegetable Soup

½ cup sliced red onion

4 cloves garlic

1 tablespoon chopped fresh ginger

1 fresh hot chili, deseeded

2 tablespoons vegetable oil

4 cups fish stock

2 cups water

4–6 tablespoons fresh lime juice

3 tablespoons minced lemongrass

2 star anise

1 cup grated carrots

1 cup sliced fresh shiitake mushrooms (stems removed)

½ cup chopped fresh or canned tomatoes

6 spring onions, sliced

fish sauce to taste (optional)

1 pound white fish fillets (e.g. snapper, orange roughy), cut into strips

½ cup fresh cilantro leaves

Process or pound onion, garlic, ginger and chili to a coarse paste. Heat oil in a largeish saucepan, add onion paste and sauté for a minute or two until fragrant. Add the stock and water, 4 tablespoons of the lime juice, the lemongrass and star anise, and bring to boil. Reduce heat, then cover and simmer for 10 minutes.

Remove star anise from the broth, add the carrots, mushrooms, tomatoes and spring onions, and fish sauce if used, then simmer for 2 minutes. Add the fish and cook for a few minutes, stirring gently, until no longer transparent. Before serving, stir in the cilantro leaves and remaining lime juice to taste.

SERVES 4–6

Mainly Chicken

Chicken soups can be a clear, flavorsome broth, perhaps with dumplings or wontons, a smooth purée, or a creamy blend brimming with vegetables and chicken pieces.

Home-made chicken soup, which was recommended as a cure for the common cold in ancient times, is still a popular comfort food all around the world. Just about every nation has evolved its own version and these are seasoned according to local tastes — ginger, spring onions, garlic and soy sauce feature in many Asian soups; herbs and wine often enliven their European counterparts. For family soups, noodles, pasta or grains are a common addition.

If you are making a clear soup, it is important to use a good-quality stock, preferably home-made.

Chicken and Corn Chowder

1 tablespoon olive oil

1 clove garlic, crushed

1 onion, finely chopped

1 teaspoon grated fresh ginger

1 potato, peeled and grated

kernels from 3 corn cobs

4 cups chicken stock

2 tablespoons dry sherry

1 cooked chicken breast, shredded

1–2 tablespoons finely chopped spring onions

2 teaspoons light soy sauce

2 teaspoons sesame seeds, toasted

Heat oil in a saucepan and add garlic, onion and ginger. Cook over a gentle heat until onion is soft. Add potato, corn and stock. Bring to a boil and simmer, uncovered, for 20 minutes until corn is tender.

Stir in sherry, chicken, spring onions and soy sauce. Cook for 4–5 minutes until chicken is heated through. Ladle soup into bowls and garnish with sesame seeds.

SERVES 4–6

Chicken Laksa

LAKSA PASTE

1 small red onion, finely chopped

6 cloves garlic, chopped

6 large dried chilies, seeds removed

1 stick lemongrass, finely chopped

1 tablespoon grated fresh ginger

12 macadamia nuts

2 tablespoons fresh cilantro leaves

1 teaspoon ground turmeric

1 teaspoon Thai shrimp paste

1–2 tablespoons peanut oil

SOUP

2 cups chicken stock

½ pound chicken breast fillet

2 cups coconut milk

2 tablespoons fish sauce

juice of 1 lime

2 cups cooked rice noodles

½ cup bean sprouts

4 small hot chilies (such as Thai), deseeded and sliced

1 tablespoon fresh cilantro leaves

1 spring onion, finely chopped

¼ cup chopped fresh mint

To make laksa paste, pound or blend all the ingredients in a spice grinder or food processor and blend together to form a rough paste. Add a little oil or chicken stock to help blend if needed. Store in a jar and refrigerate until ready to use. >

To make the soup, heat stock in a large saucepan and add chicken breast. Poach over a gentle heat for 10 minutes, remove and cool. Shred chicken into strips and set aside. Add coconut milk and laksa paste to the saucepan and bring to a boil. Simmer for 15 minutes, then add fish sauce.

Divide noodles, bean sprouts and chicken between serving bowls and ladle hot soup over. Garnish with chili slices, cilantro leaves, and chopped spring onion and mint.

Laksa paste is very easy to make and keeps well in the refrigerator. But you can substitute a good-quality bought paste, which (like Thai shrimp paste) you'll find in supermarkets and Asian food stores.

SERVES 4–6

Chicken and Mustard Soup

1 tablespoon butter or olive oil

3 leeks, sliced

3 potatoes, peeled and cut
   into chunks

3 parsnips, peeled and cut
   into chunks

3 tablespoons seeded mustard

4 cups chicken stock

7 ounces crème fraîche

½ pound cooked chicken, shredded

2 tablespoons chopped fresh chives

In a large saucepan heat butter or oil and cook leeks gently for 6–8 minutes until soft. Add potatoes, parsnips and 2 tablespoons of the mustard. Cook for 2–3 minutes, then pour in stock. Bring to a boil and simmer for 20 minutes until vegetables are tender.

Stir in crème fraîche and chicken, and heat through. Ladle into bowls and garnish with the remaining mustard and the chopped chives.

SERVES 4

Greek Egg and Lemon Soup with Chicken

2 tablespoons long-grain rice

juice of 1 lemon

3 eggs, beaten

1-1½ quarts chicken stock

1 cup shredded cooked chicken

salt and freshly ground black
    pepper

2 tablespoons finely chopped
    fresh parsley or cilantro

Heat stock in a saucepan. Add rice and simmer for 15–20 minutes until just tender.

Beat lemon juice and eggs together in a bowl until well combined. Whisk about 1 cup of the hot stock into the eggs, a little at a time, until combined. Remove saucepan from heat and slowly whisk in the egg mixture. Stir in the chicken, season to taste, then ladle into soup bowls and garnish with chopped parsley or cilantro.

🥣 You can substitute fish for the chicken, using chicken or fish stock as preferred.

SERVES 4–6

Italian Chicken and Pasta Soup

1 tablespoon olive oil

1 green pepper, deseeded and
finely chopped

1 onion, finely chopped

1 bulb fennel, finely chopped

3 cloves garlic, crushed

1 teaspoon crushed fennel seeds

3 tablespoons chopped fresh
basil (or ½ tablespoon
dried basil)

5 cups chicken stock

2/3 pound cheese tortellini

1 cup diced, cooked chicken

3 zucchini, coarsely chopped

extra 1 tablespoon shredded
fresh basil, for garnish

2–3 tablespoons grated
Parmesan cheese

In a saucepan heat oil and add pepper, onion, chopped fennel, garlic,
fennel seeds and chopped (or dried) basil. Cook over a low heat for 10–15
minutes, until vegetables are soft. Pour in stock, bring to a boil and then
add tortellini and zucchini. Simmer for a further 10 minutes, or until pasta is
just cooked. Ladle into bowls and garnish with the shredded basil and the
Parmesan cheese.

SERVES 4–6

Mexican Chicken and Bean Soup with Avocado

1 tablespoon olive oil

1 onion, finely chopped

leaves from 1 bunch fresh cilantro, finely chopped

1 small fresh red chili, deseeded and finely chopped

2 red peppers, deseeded and finely chopped

1 green pepper, deseeded and finely chopped

3 cloves garlic, crushed

2 chicken breasts

4 cups chicken stock

14 ounces canned kidney beans, drained

2 large ripe avocados, peeled and flesh cubed

juice of 1 lime

To make the soup, heat olive oil in a saucepan and add onion, three-quarters of the cilantro, and the chili, peppers and garlic. Cook over a gentle heat for 4–5 minutes until vegetables are soft, stirring occasionally.

Add chicken and 1 cup stock to the saucepan. Poach chicken for about 15 minutes until tender. Remove with tongs and shred meat with a sharp knife.

Pour remaining stock into soup and slowly bring to a boil. Stir in beans and shredded chicken to heat through. Simmer for 2–4 minutes, then stir in avocado, lime juice and remaining cilantro. Season to taste before ladling into bowls. >

Tortilla chips are a great garnish for this soup. Simply cut 4 corn tortillas into strips, then heat ½ cup vegetable oil in a frying pan. Fry tortillas strips in batches, stirring gently, until crisp and golden. Remove with tongs and drain on paper towels.

SERVES 4–6

Cock-a-leekie

1½ quarts beef stock

3 pounds chicken

6 leeks, trimmed but left whole

1 cup prunes

salt and freshly ground
black pepper

2 tablespoons chopped
fresh parsley

Heat the stock in a large pot, then add the chicken and 3 of the leeks. Simmer gently for 1½ hours, or until chicken is cooked. Remove leeks and discard. Remove chicken, slice off meat and keep warm.

Add prunes to stock, and simmer for 15 minutes. Meanwhile, slice remaining leeks, add to saucepan and simmer for about 5 minutes, until cooked but still slightly crunchy.

To serve, divide prunes, sliced leeks and chicken among heated serving bowls, and pour broth over. Season to taste with salt and pepper, and garnish with the chopped parsley.

🥣 This is a simplified version of the traditional Scottish soup, which includes beef (used to make the beef stock and then served, sliced, with the chicken). Some people omit the prunes, but this produces a quite different flavor.

SERVES 6

Mushroom Soup with Chicken Wontons

2 ounces dried shiitake mushrooms

1 tablespoon olive oil

1 teaspoon sesame oil

1 large onion, finely chopped

2 stalks celery

2 cloves garlic, crushed

4 ounces button mushrooms, sliced

4 cups chicken stock

5 ounces oyster mushrooms

4 ounces snow peas, cut into strips

4 spring onions, chopped

¼ cup dry sherry

1 tablespoon soy sauce

extra spring onions, sliced

WONTONS

⅔ pound minced chicken

1 teaspoon grated fresh ginger

1 tablespoon finely chopped fresh cilantro

2 teaspoons soy sauce

1 teaspoon toasted sesame seeds

7 ounces wonton wrappers

First make the wontons. Combine the chicken, ginger, cilantro, soy sauce and sesame seeds. Place 2 teaspoons of mixture in the center of each wonton wrapper, brush edges with water and bring opposite points together to seal edges and make a pouch. Bring a saucepan of water to a boil and cook wontons in batches for 2–3 minutes each, then drain.

To make the soup, first soak shiitake mushrooms in hot water for 30 minutes, then drain. In a large saucepan heat oils and add onion, celery, garlic and button mushrooms. Cook for 5–6 minutes until soft, then add stock. Bring to a boil and simmer for 10 minutes. Remove from heat and cool a little.

Blend soup until smooth, then return to the saucepan. Add remaining ingredients except spring onion slices, and bring back to the boil. Reduce to a simmer and add wontons to heat through.

Ladle soup into heated bowls and garnish with spring onion slices.

SERVES 4–6

Clear Soup with Chicken Wontons

WONTONS

⅓ pound minced chicken

1-inch piece fresh ginger, peeled and grated

4 spring onions finely sliced

1 tablespoon chopped fresh cilantro

1 tablespoon soy sauce

9 ounces wonton wrappers

SOUP

1 quart chicken stock

½–1 cup finely sliced spring onions, for garnish

extra soy sauce, to serve

In a small bowl, combine minced chicken with ginger, spring onions, cilantro and soy sauce. Place a teaspoon of this mixture in the middle of a wonton wrapper, wet edges, gather in the middle and then pinch together to form a little pouch. Repeat until all the chicken mixture has been used.

Bring chicken stock to a boil, add wontons, and simmer for 4–5 minutes, or until cooked through.

Serve in heated bowls, sprinkled with finely sliced spring onions. Provide extra soy sauce for guests to help themselves if desired.

SERVES 4

Noodle Soup with Peking-style Duck

1 cooked Peking duck, sliced (ask your butcher to do this for you)

1½-2 quarts chicken stock

6 dried shiitake mushrooms, soaked in 1 cup hot water

1 cup shredded Chinese cabbage

2 tablespoons light soy sauce

2 tablespoons rice wine

2 tablespoons rice vinegar

¾ pound udon (thick wheat) noodles

4 spring onions, sliced on the diagonal

½ cup bean sprouts

1 cup chopped fresh cilantro leaves

salt and freshly ground black pepper

Separate duck meat from the bones and keep warm, covered, in the oven while you make the soup. Cook noodles in boiling salted water until tender (about 5 minutes). Drain and set aside.

To assemble the soup, pour the stock into a saucepan and bring to a simmer. Add mushrooms and their soaking liquid, shredded cabbage, soy sauce, rice wine and rice vinegar, and cooked noodles. Bring to a boil and simmer for a few minutes to allow the flavors to combine.

Just before serving, scatter soup with the spring onions slices, bean sprouts and chopped cilantro. Season to taste. Ladle the soup into bowls, top with some duck pieces, and serve at once.

SERVES 4

Barley Soup with Chicken, Leek and Mushrooms

2 ounces pearl barley
juice and zest of 1 lemon
5½ cups chicken stock
1 chicken breast, thinly sliced
1–2 tablespoons butter
2 leeks, thinly sliced

4 large mushrooms, thinly sliced
½ cup white wine
salt and freshly ground black pepper
4–5 tablespoons chopped fresh parsley

Place barley, lemon juice and stock in a saucepan and slowly bring to a boil. Cover and simmer for about 40 minutes or until barley is tender. Add chicken and cook for 4–5 minutes until tender.

Meanwhile, heat butter in a frying pan and gently cook leeks and mushrooms until golden-brown. Add wine to deglaze the pan, then add the vegetables and liquid to soup. Season to taste. Add lemon zest and parsley, and check seasoning. Ladle soup into bowls, distributing chicken evenly.

SERVES 4–6

Thai Chicken and Coconut Soup

1 quart chicken stock

1 tablespoon sliced lemongrass

1 tablespoon grated fresh
galangal (see note)

1 clove garlic, crushed

3 fresh red Thai chilies,
deseeded and sliced

4 kaffir lime leaves, sliced finely

¼ teaspoon ground turmeric

2 cups coconut milk

1 tablespoon fish sauce

1 pound chicken thigh fillets,
sliced thinly

2 spring onions, chopped finely

2 tablespoons fresh lime juice

1 tablespoon chopped fresh
cilantro leaves

Heat stock in large saucepan. Add lemongrass, galangal, garlic, chilies,
lime leaves and turmeric, and simmer for 10–15 minutes until fragrant.

Stir in coconut milk and fish sauce, and bring to a boil. Add chicken and
simmer, uncovered, for about 20 minutes or until chicken is cooked through
and soup liquid reduced slightly.

Just before serving, stir in spring onions, lime juice and chopped cilantro.

🥣 If you can't find fresh galangal, substitute 1 tablespoon grated fresh
ginger or a ¾-inch piece of dried galangal (soak it in warm water before use).

SERVES 4–6

Mainly Meat

The soups in this section all have meat as the predominant flavor, though some contain relatively small quantities — often of bacon, ham or sliced sausage — to add flavor rather than bulk. Others, such as the oxtail soup, are truly hearty, meaty meals in a bowl, with their origins in simple farmhouse fare.

As with most soups, using a flavorful (preferably home-made) stock makes a world of difference, especially where clear broth is a feature of the soup.

Black-eyed Pea Soup with Chorizo

⅔ pound chorizo sausage,
  thinly sliced

1 tablespoon olive oil

1 onion, finely chopped

4 stalks celery, finely chopped

2 cloves garlic, finely chopped

1 red pepper, deseeded and
  chopped

1 pound black-eyed peas,
  soaked overnight

4 cups chicken stock

14 ounces canned tomatoes,
  with their juice

½ teaspoon dried thyme

2 bay leaves

3 carrots, peeled and chopped

salt and freshly ground
  black pepper

garlic croutons (see page 4)

chopped fresh cilantro,
  to garnish

In a saucepan brown chorizo in the oil over gentle heat for 5–6 minutes, stirring all the time. Remove with a slotted spoon. Add onion, celery, garlic and pepper to the pan. (Remove some of the fat if there is more than a tablespoon.) Cook over gentle heat for 4–5 minutes until soft. Add peas, stock, tomatoes, thyme and bay leaves and bring to a boil. Simmer, covered, for about 1 hour until peas are tender.

Stir in carrot and cooked chorizo, and cook an additional 10-15 minutes. Remove bay leaves and season well. Ladle into bowls, garnish with garlic croutons and sprinkle with the chopped cilantro.

SERVES 4

Transylvanian Sausage Soup

¼ pound lean bacon, finely
  chopped

1 onion, finely chopped

3 cloves garlic, crushed

1 pound cabbage, coarsely
  shredded

1 teaspoon ground hot paprika

freshly ground black pepper

28 ounces canned tomatoes,
  roughly chopped

3 cups chicken or vegetable stock

¼ cup raisins

1 cinnamon stick

2 bay leaves

2/3 pound knackwurst or other
  smoked sausage, cut into thin
  rounds

2 tablespoons freshly chopped
  parsley

In a large saucepan fry bacon over a gentle heat for 5 or so minutes until crisp. Add onion and garlic and cook for 4–5 minutes. Add cabbage, paprika and pepper and cook an additional 5 minutes, stirring occasionally, until cabbage is wilted.

Add tomatoes, stock, raisins, cinnamon stick and bay leaves and bring to a boil. Simmer over low heat for 45 minutes. Remove bay leaves and cinnamon stick. Add sausage and heat through. Ladle into bowls and garnish with parsley.

SERVES 4

Moroccan Lamb, Chickpea and Lentil Soup

⅓ pound chickpeas, soaked

2 tablespoons olive oil

2 red onions, finely chopped

½ pound lamb shoulder, diced

1 cup chopped fresh parsley

½ cup chopped celery leaves

1 teaspoon ground turmeric

1 teaspoon freshly ground
    black pepper

½ teaspoon ground ginger

1 teaspoon ground cinnamon

1½ quarts water

¾ cup red lentils

1 cup chopped fresh cilantro
    leaves

1 pound ripe tomatoes, peeled

1 teaspoon harissa (see page 22)

salt

juice of 1 lemon

Drain and rinse chickpeas. Heat oil in a large pot and sauté onions, lamb, half of the chopped parsley, the celery leaves, turmeric and pepper. When lamb is lightly browned, add chickpeas, ginger, cinnamon and water. Bring to a simmer, then cover and cook gently for at least 1 hour until lamb and chickpeas are tender.

Purée half of the chopped cilantro with the tomatoes and add to pot with the lentils and harissa. Cover and simmer for about 30 minutes until lentils are cooked. Taste and adjust salt if needed. Just before serving, add lemon juice and sprinkle with reserved cilantro and parsley.

SERVES 4–6

Lentil and Tomato Soup with Lamb Koftas

SOUP

2 tablespoons oil

1 onion, finely chopped

4 tomatoes, peeled, deseeded
  and roughly chopped

1 teaspoon each ground cumin,
  turmeric and coriander

¼ teaspoon ground cinnamon

1 teaspoon green chili paste

4 cups vegetable stock

⅓ pound red lentils

juice of 1 lime

salt and ground black pepper

4–6 tablespoons yogurt

½ cup fresh cilantro leaves

KOFTAS

1 pound minced lamb

1 small onion, finely chopped

2 cloves garlic, crushed

1 egg, lightly beaten

First make the koftas. Mix well together the minced lamb, onion, garlic and egg. Shape mixture into walnut-sized balls and chill until ready to use.

To make the soup, in a saucepan heat oil and add onion, tomatoes, spices and chili paste. Cook over gentle heat until tomatoes are soft and syrupy. Add stock and lentils, bring to a boil and simmer, covered, for 20 minutes.

Add koftas to the soup. Bring back to a boil and simmer an additional 15-20 minutes until lentils and koftas are cooked. Stir in lime juice and season to taste.

Ladle into soup bowls and garnish with a dollop of yogurt and some cilantro leaves.

SERVES 4 – 6

Borscht with Bacon

1 tablespoon olive oil

¼ pound lean bacon, finely
chopped

1⅔ pounds fresh beets, peeled
and coarsely grated, leaves
shredded

2 carrots, peeled and coarsely
grated

1 large onion, finely chopped

3 stalks celery, cut into
matchstick strips

5 cups beef stock

1 tablespoon wine vinegar

½ pound tomatoes, deseeded
and chopped

salt and freshly ground
black pepper

5 ounces crème fraîche

½ cup chopped dill pickles
(optional)

In a large saucepan heat oil and add bacon. Cook for 3–4 minutes over
gentle heat, then add grated beets, carrots, onion and celery. Cook over
low heat, stirring occasionally, for 4–5 minutes.

Pour in stock, vinegar and tomatoes, and season to taste. Cover, bring
to a boil and then simmer for 30 minutes, or until vegetables are just
cooked. Add shredded beet leaves and simmer an additional 10 minutes.
Ladle into soup bowls and garnish with crème fraîche, and dill pickles if
desired.

SERVES 4–6

Asian-style Beef and Noodle Soup

½ pound fillet of beef

2 tablespoons teriyaki sauce

1–2 tablespoons vegetable oil

1 pound fresh ramen noodles

5 cups beef or chicken stock

1 tablespoon hot chili sauce

1 tablespoon fish sauce

1 tablespoon dry sherry

1 tablespoon sweet soy sauce
(kecap manis)

juice of 1 lime

4 red chilies, deseeded and
cut into thin strips

4 spring onions, finely chopped

4 sprigs fresh mint

4 ounces bean sprouts

Marinate beef in teriyaki sauce for 15 minutes. Boil noodles for 2–3 minutes, then drain.

Heat oil in a frying pan and cook beef for 4–5 minutes on each side. Remove, cut into thin slices and keep warm.

In a saucepan heat stock, chili sauce, fish sauce, sherry and sweet soy sauce and bring to a boil. Stir in lime juice.

Place equal amounts of noodles in each bowl and ladle soup over. Top with beef slices, chilies, spring onions, mint and bean sprouts.

SERVES 4–6

Split Pea Soup with Ham

1 tablespoon butter

1 onion, finely chopped

2 cloves garlic, finely chopped

¼ pound Prosciutto or Pancetta, finely chopped

1 bay leaf

½ cup yellow split peas, washed and picked over

½ cup green split peas, washed and picked over

6 cups water

1 teaspoon salt

¼ teaspoon freshly ground pepper

½ cup finely chopped fresh parsley

½ cup croutons (see page 4), for garnish

In a saucepan melt butter and cook onion and garlic until soft. Stir in ham and cook for 2–3 minutes.

Add bay leaf, split peas, water, salt and pepper. Bring to a boil, cover and then simmer for 45 minutes or so until split peas are cooked and soup has thickened.

Remove bay leaf and stir in chopped parsley. Ladle soup into bowls and garnish with croutons.

SERVES 4–6

Oxtail Soup with Red Wine

½ cup olive oil

3⅓ POUNDS meaty oxtails, patted dry

salt and pepper

2 quarts beef or chicken stock

3 cups red wine

bouquet garni

2 onions, chopped

2 leeks (white and pale-green parts only), chopped

3 carrots, finely chopped

2 parsnips, finely chopped

6 cloves garlic, finely chopped

1 teaspoon dried thyme

1 bay leaf

2 large potatoes, peeled and diced

½ cup finely chopped flat-leaf parsley

Heat 2–3 tablespoons of the oil in a large pot over medium heat. Sprinkle oxtails with salt and pepper, add to the pot and brown on all sides. Add the stock, 2 cups of the wine, plus the bouquet garni. Bring to boil, cover partially and simmer gently until meat is very tender and falling off the bones (2–3 hours).

Using tongs, transfer oxtails to a large bowl. Strain the cooking liquid into another bowl, and spoon off any fat. Remove meat from the bones, and discard the bones. >

Heat remaining oil in large pot over medium heat. Add onions, leeks, carrots, parsnips, garlic, thyme and bay leaf. Sauté until vegetables are golden (about 10 minutes).

Add strained cooking liquid, oxtail meat, remaining wine, and potatoes to the pot. Bring to boil, cover, and simmer for another 10 minutes, or until vegetables are tender. Remove bay leaf.

Serve garnished with the chopped parsley.

SERVES 4–6

Scotch Broth

2 pounds lamb breast or neck,
   trimmed of excess fat

2 tablespoons pearl barley

8 cups water

1 slice bacon, chopped

1 tablespoon butter

½ cup diced carrot

½ cup diced turnip

½ cup finely chopped onion

½ cup peas

¼ cup finely sliced cabbage

chopped parsley, to serve

salt and freshly ground
   black pepper

Put lamb and barley in a large pot, cover with the water, bring to a boil and simmer for 1½ hours or until meat is very tender. Remove meat from stock and discard bones. Allow stock to cool, then spoon off any fat.

In a fresh pot, fry the bacon in butter until the fat melts, then add the carrot, turnip, onion, peas and cabbage, and sauté for 10 minutes. Add stock and meat, bring to boil and simmer for 5–10 minutes or until vegetables are tender. Stir in parsley, salt and pepper just before serving.

SERVES 6

Meaty Minestrone with Parmesan Dumplings

3 tablespoons olive oil

1 onion, chopped

3 carrots, peeled and cut into chunks

1 bulb fennel, chopped

1 small red pepper, deseeded and cut into strips

¼ pound green beans, chopped

¼ head cabbage, finely shredded

4 cups beef stock

4 ounces red wine

14 ounces canned tomatoes

2 teaspoons dried oregano

2 fresh Italian sausages, chopped

4 ounces canned kidney beans

2 tablespoons chopped fresh basil

salt and ground black pepper

freshly grated Parmesan cheese

DUMPLINGS

2 slices white bread, crusts removed

3 tablespoons freshly grated Parmesan cheese

pinch of dry mustard

salt and freshly ground black pepper

1 egg, lightly beaten

First make the dumplings. Blend or process bread into fine crumbs, stir in Parmesan cheese and dry mustard, and season to taste. Mix in enough egg to bind mixture. Roll into small balls and chill until ready to use.

For the soup, first heat oil in a large pot and add onion. Cook over a low heat until soft. Add carrots, fennel, pepper and green beans and cook, stirring, for 3–4 minutes. Add cabbage and cook for 5 minutes, stirring occasionally. Add stock, red wine, tomatoes and their juice, and oregano. Slowly bring to a boil and simmer for 35–40 minutes until vegetables are just tender.

Stir in chopped sausages, drained kidney beans and basil. Cook for 3–4 minutes and then drop in dumplings. Cook for 1–2 minutes until dumplings are firm. Season to taste. Ladle into bowls and garnish with Parmesan cheese.

SERVES 4–6

Cabbage and Bacon Soup

2 tablespoons olive oil
2 cloves garlic, chopped
2 leeks, finely chopped
3 slices bacon, finely chopped
½ head cabbage, shredded
3–4 cups chicken stock
salt and freshly ground black pepper
3 tablespoons finely chopped fresh parsley

Heat the olive oil in a saucepan over medium heat. Add the garlic and leeks and sauté for 2–3 minutes. Add the chopped bacon and sauté for another few minutes until bacon has browned a little. Add the cabbage and fry, stirring regularly, for 2–3 minutes, until soft.

Add the chicken stock and bring to a boil, then reduce the heat and simmer for 10 minutes. Blend the soup to a coarse purée and season to taste with salt and pepper.

Serve garnished with the chopped parsley.

SERVES 4

Purée Soups

Purée soups, which may be subtle or substantial, have a naturally creamy texture (though occasionally thickeners such as flour may be included). For contrast, these soups are often garnished with crunchy bits such as croutons or nuts. A swirl of cream or yogurt or a scattering of herbs turns a simple purée into something special.

For puréeing soups, a blender is generally preferable to a food processor as it gives a smoother result. For a coarser, rustic texture, simply blend the soup for a shorter time until you achieve the consistency you want.

Leftover vegetables, especially if roasted or grilled, make a great base for quick purée soups. All you need to do is cook a little fresh onion and garlic in oil, perhaps add some chopped fresh herbs and a splash of wine. Add the leftover veggies, top up with stock, reheat gently and blend contents.

Curried Carrot Soup

1 tablespoon vegetable oil

1–2 teaspoons curry powder

1 onion, finely chopped

1 tablespoon chopped fresh
  ginger

1 pound carrots, peeled
  and thinly sliced

4 cups chicken or vegetable stock

2 tablespoons lemon juice

salt and freshly ground
  black pepper

yogurt, to serve

½ cup chopped fresh parsley
  or cilantro

Heat oil in a saucepan and add curry powder, onion and ginger. Cook until onion is soft. Add carrots and cook, covered, for 20 minutes, stirring from time to time. Pour in stock and bring to a boil. Simmer for 15 minutes or until carrots are tender.

Blend soup until smooth. Return to the saucepan and gently reheat. Stir in lemon juice and season to taste. Ladle into bowls and garnish with a swirl of yogurt and the chopped parsley or cilantro.

SERVES 4–6

Grilled Pepper Soup with Cilantro Pesto

SOUP

2 red peppers

1 tablespoon olive oil

1 onion, finely chopped

2 cloves garlic, finely chopped

14 ounces canned tomatoes

4 cups vegetable stock

1 teaspoon shredded lemon zest

juice of 1 lemon

2 teaspoons sugar

salt and freshly ground
   black pepper

PESTO

$1\frac{1}{2}$ cups chopped fresh cilantro
   leaves

$1\frac{1}{2}$ cups chopped fresh parsley

2 cloves garlic, crushed

$\frac{1}{2}$ cup roasted cashew nuts

$\frac{1}{2}$ cup freshly grated
   Parmesan cheese

3–4 tablespoons olive oil

Cut peppers in half and remove pith and seeds. Grill until skins are blistered and blackened. Remove to a plastic bag and leave for 5 minutes. When cool, remove skins and finely chop flesh.

In a saucepan heat oil and add onion and garlic. Cook over gentle heat for 3–4 minutes. Add peppers, tomatoes (with their juice) and stock. Bring to a boil and simmer for 15–20 minutes. Remove from heat and cool a little. Add lemon zest and juice, sugar, salt and pepper. >

Meanwhile, make the cilantro pesto. Blend first five ingredients in a food processor, then gradually add oil until a smooth, creamy sauce forms.

Blend soup in batches until smooth (or leave a little chunky, for a rustic touch). Check seasoning and return soup to the pan.

Ladle into bowls and garnish with cilantro pesto.

SERVES 4–6

Tomato and Orange Soup

2 tablespoons olive oil

1 onion, finely chopped

2 cloves garlic, finely chopped

2 pounds ripe tomatoes, roughly
chopped

salt and freshly ground
black pepper

1 bay leaf

4 cups chicken or vegetable stock

zest and juice of 1 orange

2 tablespoons chopped
fresh parsley

In a saucepan heat oil and add onion and garlic. Cook over gentle heat until soft. Add tomatoes, salt, pepper and bay leaf, then pour in stock. Slowly bring to a boil and cook, covered, for 15–20 minutes until tomatoes are soft.

Remove from heat, discard bay leaf and cool soup a little. Blend soup until smooth. Sieve back into the saucepan and add orange zest and juice. Gently reheat and check seasoning. Ladle into bowls and garnish with chopped parsley.

SERVES 4–6

Creamy Tomato Soup

1 tablespoon butter

1 onion, finely chopped

2 cloves garlic, crushed

1 potato, peeled and thinly
  sliced

1 pound tomatoes, roughly
  chopped

1 bay leaf

2 tablespoons tomato paste

4 cups vegetable stock

salt and freshly ground
  black pepper

½ cup crème fraîche

1 tablespoon finely chopped
  fresh parsley

In a saucepan melt butter and add onion and garlic. Cook over gentle heat until soft. Add potato, tomatoes, bay leaf, tomato paste and stock. Bring to a boil and simmer, covered, for about 20 minutes until potato is tender.

Blend contents of pan until smooth. Return to the saucepan and gently reheat. Stir in crème fraîche. Ladle into bowls and garnish with chopped parsley.

SERVES 4–6

Spiced Parsnip Soup

1 tablespoon oil

1 onion, finely chopped

1 leek, thinly sliced

½ teaspoon sugar

½ teaspoon finely grated fresh ginger

¼ teaspoon ground turmeric

pinch of ground nutmeg

1 pound parsnips, peeled and thinly sliced

1 potato, peeled and thinly sliced

3 cups chicken stock

salt and freshly ground black pepper

½ cup creamy yogurt

1 tablespoon chopped pistachio nuts

Heat oil in a large saucepan and add onion, leek, sugar, ginger, turmeric and nutmeg. Cook until onion and leek are soft. Add parsnips and potato and cook, covered an additional 5 minutes over a low heat. Pour in stock and bring to a boil. Simmer for 30 minutes or until vegetables are tender.

Blend contents of saucepan until smooth. Return to pan and gently reheat. Season to taste. Ladle into bowls, swirl in a little yogurt and garnish with the chopped pistachios.

SERVES 4–6

Cauliflower and Swiss Cheese Soup

1 tablespoon butter or oil

1 onion, finely chopped

2 cloves garlic, crushed

1 large potato, peeled and
thinly sliced

1 medium cauliflower, cut into
small florets

3 cups vegetable stock

1 heaped tablespoon grainy
mustard

½ cup crème fraîche or cream

salt and freshly ground
black pepper

2 cups croutons (see page 4)

¼ cup grated Swiss cheese

In a saucepan melt butter or heat oil, and add onion and garlic. Cook over
gentle heat until soft. Add potato and cauliflower, sauté for a few minutes
and then pour in stock. Slowly bring to a boil and cook, covered, for 15–20
minutes until vegetables are tender. Remove from heat and cool a little.

Place in a blender or food processor and purée until smooth. Return to the
saucepan and gently reheat. Stir in mustard and crème fraîche or cream.
Season to taste. Ladle into bowls, toss a few croutons over the top and
sprinkle with a little cheese.

SERVES 4–6

Indian Mushroom Soup

2 tablespoons olive oil

1 onion, finely chopped

1 carrot, finely chopped

2 stalks celery, finely chopped

2 cloves garlic, crushed

½ teaspoon ground turmeric

¼ teaspoon cayenne pepper

1 teaspoon ground cumin

2 teaspoons crushed
   cardamom seeds

2 bay leaves

1 pound flat field mushrooms
   (such as Portobello or brown
   crimini), stalks removed and
   flesh roughly chopped

4 cups chicken or vegetable stock

2 tablespoons finely chopped
   fresh cilantro

½ cup creamy yogurt

8 cooked pappadums
   (Indian flatbreads)

In a large saucepan heat oil and add onion, carrot, celery, garlic, spices and bay leaves. Cook over gentle heat for 4–5 minutes until soft. Add mushrooms and cook for 6–8 minutes, stirring occasionally. Pour in stock and bring to a boil. Simmer for 15 minutes until mushrooms are cooked. Remove from heat and cool a little. Discard bay leaves.

Blend soup until smooth. Return to the saucepan and stir in the chopped cilantro. Ladle soup into bowls and serve with a dollop of yogurt and garnish with pappadum pieces.

SERVES 4–6

Button Mushroom Soup

2–3 tablespoons butter

½ pound button mushrooms,
   roughly chopped

1 onion, finely chopped

1 tablespoon all-purpose flour

4 cups chicken stock

½ cup medium sherry

5 ounces milk

salt and freshly ground
   black pepper

½ cup croutons (see page 4)

In a saucepan melt butter and add mushrooms and onion. Cook over low heat for 10 minutes, until soft. Stir in flour and cook for 1–2 minutes. Stir in stock a little at a time and slowly bring to a boil. Simmer for 15 minutes, then remove from heat and cool a little.

Blend soup until smooth. Return to the saucepan and stir in sherry. Gently cook for 5 minutes. Stir in milk and season to taste. Ladle into bowls and garnish with croutons.

SERVES 4–6

Turnip and Pear Soup

2 tablespoons olive oil

1 onion, finely chopped

3 white turnips, peeled and finely
  chopped

3 ripe pears, peeled, cored and
  finely chopped

4 cups chicken or vegetable stock

1 teaspoon fresh lemon thyme

salt and freshly ground black pepper

1 tablespoon finely chopped
  fresh mint

In a saucepan heat oil and add onion, turnips and pears. Cook over gentle heat for 3–4 minutes. Pour in stock, add lemon thyme and bring to a boil. Simmer, covered, until vegetables are tender. Remove from heat and cool a little.

Blend contents of pan until smooth. Return to the saucepan and gently reheat. Season to taste. Ladle soup into bowls and garnish with the chopped mint.

SERVES 4–6

Pear, Pea and Watercress Soup

1 tablespoon butter

1 small onion, finely chopped

1 pound firm pears, peeled, cored and finely sliced

2 pounds fresh peas, shelled (or use 1⅔ pounds frozen peas)

½ cup dry sherry

¼ teaspoon salt

¼ teaspoon ground white pepper

pinch of ground mace

4 cups chicken stock

2 bunches watercress, stalks removed

2 fresh or dried pears, thinly sliced

In a large saucepan melt butter and add onion, pears and peas. Cook for 2–3 minutes over gentle heat. Add sherry and seasonings and cook, covered, for 20 minutes over low heat. Add stock and watercress and bring to a boil. Simmer for 15 minutes, then remove from heat and cool a little.

Blend soup until smooth, then sieve back into the saucepan. Gently reheat. Ladle into bowls and garnish with slices of pear.

SERVES 4–6

Mushroom and Almond Soup

1–2 tablespoons butter

1 onion, finely chopped

2 cloves garlic, crushed

½ teaspoon dried thyme

½ pound mushrooms, roughly
chopped

3 cups vegetable stock

1 cup milk

½ cup roasted, chopped
almonds

salt and freshly ground
black pepper

1 tablespoon almond slices

In a saucepan melt butter and add onion and garlic. Cook over gentle heat until soft. Add thyme and mushrooms and cook for 3–4 minutes. Add stock and bring to a boil. Simmer, covered, for about 20 minutes. Stir in milk and almonds. Remove from heat and cool a little.

Blend contents of saucepan until smooth. Return to the saucepan and gently reheat. Season to taste. Ladle into bowls and garnish with almond slices.

SERVES 4–6

Apple, Pecan and Blue Cheese Soup

1 tablespoon butter

1 onion, finely chopped

2 stalks celery, finely chopped

4 Granny Smith apples, peeled, cored and thinly sliced

4 cups chicken stock

⅓ pound blue cheese

½ cup cream

½ cup white wine

½ cup finely chopped pecans

salt and freshly ground black pepper

2 tablespoons chopped fresh chives

In a saucepan heat butter and add onion, celery and apples. Cook over gentle heat until soft. Add stock and bring to a boil. Simmer for 20 minutes. Remove from heat and cool a little.

Blend soup with the blue cheese until smooth. Return to the saucepan and stir in cream, white wine and pecans. Season to taste. Gently reheat, then ladle into bowls and serve garnished with chives.

SERVES 4–6

Cream of Fennel Soup

2 tablespoons olive oil

1 large onion, finely chopped

2 bulbs fennel, finely chopped

salt and freshly ground black
    pepper

½ teaspoon fennel seeds

4 cups chicken stock

½ cup crème fraîche

1 cup garlic croutons (page 4),
    for garnish

In a saucepan heat oil and add onion and fennel. Cook over gentle heat for 8–10 minutes, stirring occasionally. Season to taste and add fennel seeds. Pour in stock and bring to a boil. Simmer, covered, until fennel is tender. Remove from heat and cool a little.

Blend contents of saucepan until smooth. Return to the saucepan and gently reheat. Check seasoning. Stir in crème fraîche just before serving. Garnish with croutons.

SERVES 4–6

Curried Apple and Celery Soup

1 tablespoon oil

2 onions, finely chopped

2 stalks celery, finely chopped

2 large Granny Smith apples,
   peeled, cored and finely
   chopped

2 tablespoons all-purpose flour

2 tablespoons curry powder

4 cups chicken stock

salt and freshly ground
   black pepper

½ cup yogurt

1 tablespoon finely chopped
   fresh chives

Heat oil in a large saucepan and add onions, celery and apples. Cook for
3–4 minutes, then stir in flour and curry powder. Cook for 2 minutes, then
slowly pour in stock. Slowly bring to a boil and simmer, uncovered, for
20 minutes until vegetables are tender. Remove from heat and cool a little.

Blend soup until smooth. Return to the saucepan and gently reheat.
Season to taste. Ladle into bowls and garnish with a little yogurt and
chopped chives.

SERVES 4–6

Broccoli Stalk Soup

1 tablespoon butter

2 leeks, thinly sliced

2 cloves garlic, finely chopped

2 pounds broccoli stalks, trimmed
   and thinly sliced

1 large potato, thinly sliced

3 cups chicken or vegetable stock

salt and freshly ground black pepper

7 ounces crème fraîche

1 cup croutons (see page 4)

½ teaspoon lemon pepper
   seasoning

In a saucepan melt butter and add leeks and garlic. Cook over gentle heat until soft. Add broccoli stalks and potato and pour in stock. Slowly bring to a boil and cook, covered, for 15–20 minutes until vegetables are tender. Remove from heat and cool a little.

Blend soup until smooth. Return to the saucepan and gently reheat. Stir in crème fraîche. Season to taste. Ladle into bowls, toss a few croutons over the top and sprinkle with a little lemon pepper seasoning.

SERVES 4–6

Celery Root, Leek and Apple Soup with Ginger

1 tablespoon oil

2 leeks, roughly chopped

1 celery root, peeled and roughly chopped (approximately 1 pound)

2 Granny Smith apples, peeled, cored and chopped

1 tablespoon chopped fresh ginger

juice of 1 lime

3 cups chicken or vegetable stock

1 cup milk

salt and freshly ground black pepper

2–3 tablespoons crème fraîche

1 tablespoon chopped fresh chives

In a saucepan heat oil and add leeks, celery root, apples and ginger. Cook over low heat for 10 minutes, stirring occasionally, until vegetables are soft. Stir in lime juice and stock and slowly bring to a boil. Simmer for 5 minutes, then remove from heat and cool a little.

Blend soup until smooth. Return to the saucepan and gently reheat. Stir in milk and season to taste. Ladle into bowls with a swirl of crème fraîche and a few chopped chives for garnish.

SERVES 4–6

Spinach and Walnut Soup

1 tablespoon butter

1 onion, finely chopped

2 stalks celery, finely chopped

2 potatoes, peeled and thinly
   sliced

3 cups chicken stock

1 large bunch spinach, stalks
   removed and leaves shredded

pinch of ground nutmeg

½ cup chopped walnuts

¼ cup crème fraîche or cream

walnut halves, to serve

In a large saucepan melt butter and add onion, celery and potatoes. Cook for 3–4 minutes. Add stock and bring to a boil. Simmer for 20 minutes until potato is tender. Add spinach leaves to soup for last 2–3 minutes of cooking time. Remove from heat and cool a little.

Place in a blender and purée until smooth. Return to the saucepan and gently reheat. Add nutmeg and season to taste. Stir in walnuts and crème fraîche just before serving. Ladle into bowls and garnish with walnut halves.

SERVES 4–6

Spicy Pumpkin Soup

1 tablespoon olive oil

1 large onion, finely chopped

2 cloves garlic, crushed

1 tablespoon finely grated
   fresh ginger

½ teaspoon ground turmeric

1 pound butternut squash
   (also known as butternut
   pumpkin), peeled and cut
   into chunks

3 cups chicken stock

½ cup coconut cream

1 tablespoon sweet chili sauce

1 teaspoon grated lemon zest

salt and freshly ground
   black pepper

1 tablespoon shredded coconut

Heat oil in a large saucepan over a low heat and add onion, garlic, ginger, turmeric and pumpkin. Cook for 4–5 minutes, then add stock and bring to a boil. Simmer, covered, for 20–30 minutes until pumpkin is tender. Remove from heat and cool a little.

Blend soup until smooth. Return to the saucepan and gently reheat. Stir in coconut cream, sweet chili sauce and lemon zest. Season to taste. Ladle into bowls and garnish with shredded coconut.

SERVES 4–6

Onion Soup with Feta Cheese

2 tablespoons oil

2 large onions, thinly sliced

4 cloves garlic, finely chopped

2 tablespoons all-purpose flour

3 cups beef stock

6 ounces dry white wine

4 ounces cream or milk

salt and freshly ground
 black pepper

1 cup croutons (see page 4)

4 ounces feta cheese, crumbled

In a saucepan heat oil and add onions and garlic. Cook over gentle heat until soft, stirring occasionally, being careful not to brown. Stir in flour and cook for 2 minutes, then slowly pour in stock and wine. Continue stirring until soup comes to a boil, then simmer for 15–20 minutes until slightly thickened. Remove from heat and cool a little.

Blend contents of saucepan until smooth. Return to the pan and gently reheat. Stir in cream or milk and season to taste.. Ladle into bowls and garnish with croutons and feta cheese.

SERVES 4–6

Cauliflower Soup with Blue Cheese

1 medium-sized cauliflower

1½ quarts water

2 bay leaves

large pinch of salt

1 tablespoon butter

1 onion, chopped

2 stalks celery, chopped

1 leek, chopped

1 large potato, peeled and diced

2-3 tablespoons Roquefort or mild blue cheese, crumbled

2–3 tablespoons crème fraîche

salt and freshly ground black pepper

snipped fresh chives, to serve

To make the stock, separate the cauliflower into florets and set these aside. Place stalks and green stems in a medium-sized saucepan. Add water, bay leaves and salt, bring to a boil, cover, and simmer for 20 minutes.

Meanwhile, melt the butter in a large saucepan. Add onion, celery, leek and potato, cover and sweat the vegetables for 10–15 minutes. When the stock is ready, strain it into the pan containing the vegetables (include the bay leaves but discard the cauliflower trimmings). Add the cauliflower florets, bring stock to boil and then simmer very gently for 20–25 minutes, until the cauliflower is completely tender. >

Remove the bay leaves, then blend the contents of the pan until smooth and creamy. Return it to the saucepan, stir in the blue cheese and crème fraîche, and stir until the cheese has melted and the soup is hot (do not boil). Check the seasoning, then serve in hot bowls, garnished with a little more crème fraîche, if you like, and the chives.

SERVES 4–6

Lettuce Soup

3 tablespoons butter

1 small head lettuce, shredded

2 spring onions, chopped

grated zest of ½ lemon

1 sprig fresh chervil, thyme
   or savory

4 cups chicken stock

lemon juice to taste

2 egg yolks, beaten

½ cup cream

Melt the butter in a pan and add the lettuce, spring onions, lemon zest and herbs. Cook gently for about 5 minutes, add the stock, and simmer for another 10–20 minutes.

Purée contents of pan in a blender, then return to pan to reheat. Add lemon juice, egg yolks and cream, and whisk until thickened (do not let the soup boil again, as it will curdle).

SERVES 4–6

Carrot Soup with Orange

2 tablespoons butter

1 small onion, chopped

1 stalk celery, chopped

1 sprig fresh chervil or thyme

1⅔ pounds carrots, peeled and chopped

6 cups chicken stock

salt and pepper

a little ground nutmeg

½ cup orange juice

1 tablespoon grated orange zest

cream for serving

Melt the butter in a large pan, add the onion and celery, and cook gently for 5 minutes. Add the chervil or thyme and the carrots, cover the pan and continue to cook very gently an additional 10 minutes, shaking the pan occasionally to prevent the contents sticking. Add the stock and seasoning, and simmer until tender (about 20 minutes).

Blend soup until smooth, return to the pan and stir in the orange juice and zest. Reheat, and serve with a dollop of cream in each bowl.

SERVES 6

Welsh Leek and Potato Soup

1½ tablespoons butter

4 leeks, sliced

1⅔ pounds potatoes, peeled and chopped

1 onion, chopped

6 cups chicken stock

1 cup cream

¼ teaspoon ground nutmeg

salt and pepper

3 tablespoons finely chopped fresh parsley

a few chives, snipped into 1-inch lengths

Melt the butter in a large saucepan, add the leeks, potatoes and onion, and cook over low heat until the onion is transparent. Add stock and simmer gently for about 20 minutes or until potato is tender. Blend the vegetables with some or all of the stock (depending on the consistency preferred), then stir in the cream and seasonings. Top with parsley and chives before serving.

SERVES 4–6

French Farmhouse Vegetable Soup

2 tablespoons butter

1 onion, sliced

2 carrots, peeled and diced

2 small white turnips, peeled
  and diced

2 potatoes, peeled and diced

1 cup shelled fresh peas

2 leeks, sliced

3 medium cabbage leaves, diced

2 stalks celery, diced

1 tablespoon finely chopped
  fresh thyme

2 tablespoons finely chopped
  fresh parsley

8 cups chicken or vegetable stock

salt and pepper

cream or extra butter, to serve

Melt the butter and sauté the onion in a pan until soft, then add the other vegetables. Stir continuously for about 5 minutes, then add the herbs and the stock. Bring to a boil, season, cover and simmer gently for 30–45 minutes, until root vegetables are cooked.

Blend the contents of the pan, taste again for seasoning, and serve hot, either with a little cream or 1-2 tablespoons of butter in each bowl.

SERVES 6

Leek and Onion Soup with Cheese

1 tablespoon olive oil

1 white onion, chopped

3 leeks, sliced

2 cloves garlic, chopped

1 litre chicken or vegetable stock

2 tablespoons feta or mild blue
  cheese, crumbled

finely chopped fresh chervil,
  parsley or thyme, to serve

Heat oil in a large pot. Add onion, leeks and garlic, and sauté gently until soft but not colored (5–10 minutes). Pour in stock, bring to a boil and then simmer an additional 10 minutes or so, until vegetables are tender.

Add the cheese, and stir over very low heat until melted. Purée soup in a blender until smooth.

Serve in heated bowls, sprinkled with the chopped herbs.

SERVES 4

Celery Root and Leek Soup

1 celery root

lemon juice

3 tablespoon butter

3 leeks, sliced

1 medium potato, peeled
   and roughly chopped

4–5 cups chicken or vegetable stock

half-and-half (optional)

salt and freshly ground pepper

Peel and chop celery root into small cubes and place in some water to which a little lemon juice has been added (to prevent discoloring).

Melt butter in large pan, stir in the leeks and cook until wilted. Drain celeriac and add to the pan with the potato. Add the stock and bring to boil, then reduce the heat, cover and simmer for about 20 minutes, or until tender.

Blend the contents of the pan. Stir in a couple of tablespoons of half-and-half if you wish, season with salt and pepper.

SERVES 4

Potato and Celery Root Soup

1 pound celery root

1 leek, sliced

3 tablespoons olive oil

1 pound potatoes, peeled
and chopped

1-1½ quarts chicken stock

1 tablespoon fresh thyme leaves

2 bay leaves

salt and freshly ground black
pepper

½ cup cream

finely chopped fresh parsley,
to serve

Peel the celery root, chop into chunks and drop these into water with a little lemon juice added (this stops the flesh discoloring).

In a large saucepan gently sauté the leek in 1 tablespoon of the olive oil for about 5 minutes, until soft but not colored. Add the drained celery root, potatoes and stock, and bring to a boil. Add the herbs, then simmer for 30 minutes or so until vegetables are tender. Remove the herbs, then purée the contents of the pan in a blender. Season carefully to taste, and stir in the cream.

Serve in heated bowls, sprinkled with a little chopped parsley.

SERVES 4–6

Cream of Zucchini Soup

2–3 tablespoons olive oil

1 medium-sized onion, sliced

1–2 cloves garlic, sliced

pinch of celery seeds

1⅔ pounds zucchini, sliced thickly

1 tablespoon fresh herb leaves,
    especially thyme or savory

1½–2 quarts chicken or vegetable stock

cream and snipped chives,
    to serve

Heat oil in a large saucepan. Sauté onion, garlic, and celery seeds gently for 5–10 minutes, or until softened and beginning to color. Add zucchini, toss gently for 5 minutes and then add the herbs and stock. Simmer until zucchini are tender.

Blend the contents of the pan to your preferred consistency. Serve in heated bowls, with a dollop of cream and a few snipped chives.

SERVES 4–6

Corn Chowder

1 onion, diced

3 cloves garlic, crushed

1–2 tablespoons olive oil

2 stalks celery, diced

1 carrot, peeled and diced

1 potato, peeled and diced

½ sweet potato, peeled
and diced

6 corn cobs

1 quart vegetable or chicken
stock

½ teaspoon chili flakes

chopped fresh parsley and
freshly ground pepper,
to garnish

Sauté the onion and garlic in the oil for 5 minutes in a large saucepan. Add celery, carrot, potato and sweet potato, and sauté an additional 5 minutes.

Meanwhile, boil the corn cobs in a large pot of salted water for 5 minutes. Remove the cobs, reserving 1 cup of the cooking water. Use a knife to cut the kernels from the cobs.

Add the corn kernels, stock, chili and reserved cooking water to the vegetables in the pan. Bring to a boil, then simmer for 20 minutes or until the vegetables are soft. Purée the soup to the desired consistency.

Serve garnished with chopped parsley and freshly ground pepper.

SERVES 4–6

Carrot and Cilantro Soup

1 tablespoon coriander seeds

1 tablespoon butter

2 pounds carrots, peeled
and chopped

1 clove garlic, chopped

1½ quarts chicken or vegetable
stock

salt and freshly ground
black pepper

3 tablespoons chopped fresh
cilantro

3 tablespoons sour cream
or yogurt

Toast the coriander seeds in a small pan until they begin to toast and smell fragrant. Crush them roughly.

Heat the butter in a large pan, add the carrots, garlic and half the crushed coriander seeds. Cover the pan and cook over gentle heat for 5–10 minutes, or until carrots begin to soften.

Add the stock, season with salt and pepper, and bring to a boil. Reduce the heat and simmer, partially covered, for about 15 minutes or until carrots are cooked. ➤

Blend the contents of the pan until smooth (it's also good if you leave the purée with some texture).

When ready to serve, return soup to the pan, stir in the chopped coriander and 2 tablespoons of the sour cream. Reheat, then serve garnished with a swirl of the remaining sour cream and a sprinkle of remaining crushed coriander seeds.

SERVES 6

Potato, Leek and Artichoke Soup

3 tablespoons olive oil

1 large onion, chopped

2 pounds Jerusalem artichokes, peeled
and chopped

2 pounds potatoes, peeled and chopped

2 leeks, sliced

½ cup white wine

1½ quarts chicken or vegetable stock

salt and freshly ground pepper

finely chopped fresh parsley,
mint or chervil, to serve

Heat oil gently in a large pan. Add the onion, artichokes, potatoes and leeks, and sauté for about 5 minutes or until vegetables begin to soften. Add wine to the pan, raise heat and allow to simmer for a minute or two. Lower heat again, add stock and season with salt and pepper. Simmer for about 30 minutes or until vegetables are quite tender.

Blend contents of pan to a slightly chunky purée. Season with more salt and pepper if needed. Serve with a sprinkling of the chopped herbs.

This soup is also delicious served cold, with a swirl of cream.

SERVES 4–6

Chilled Soups

Cold soups are simple to prepare, hydrate the body and refresh and titillate the palate. Best of all they can be made ahead and refrigerated, then brought out at the last minute for a super-quick meal on a hot day.

Summer vegetables such as tomatoes — watery, acid yet with a touch of sweetness — are perfect for cold soups and look wonderful too. Cucumber is another favorite. But as with soups generally, there are as many varieties of cold soup as there are regional cuisines.

Chilled fruit soups have long been popular in Baltic and eastern European countries. They were typically made of fresh summer fruits such as berries, fruits with pits and melons, or dried produce from the previous year.

Purées of young summer vegetables such as asparagus, zucchini, leeks, peas or watercress also make fine cold soups.

Classic Gazpacho

1½ cups fresh white breadcrumbs

1 cup coarsely chopped fresh tomatoes

1 small red onion, roughly chopped

1 cup chopped cucumber (peeled and deseeded first)

1 cup coarsely chopped red pepper, pith and seeds removed

2 tablespoons olive oil

¼ cup sherry

salt and freshly ground black pepper

2 tablespoons finely chopped green pepper

extra 2 tablespoons finely chopped red pepper

extra 2 tablespoons finely chopped cucumber, (deseeded and peeled)

1 tablespoon finely chopped stuffed olives

extra 2 tablespoons finely chopped red onion

½ cup croutons (see page 4)

Place breadcrumbs in a sieve and pour 2 cups cold water over. Drain any excess water and place breadcrumbs in a food processor. Add tomatoes, onion, cucumber, red pepper, oil and sherry, and blend. Season to taste. Chill until ready to serve. >

Meanwhile, in a small bowl combine the finely chopped pepper, cucumber, olives and onion. Mix well.

Ladle soup into bowls and garnish with vegetable mixture and croutons. Add an ice cube or two just before serving to chill, though this will dilute the flavors.

SERVES 4–6

Sorrel and Pea Soup

3 leeks, chopped

1½ tablespoons olive oil

1 potato, peeled and roughly
  chopped

4 cups chicken stock

1 cup fresh peas (or use thawed
  frozen peas)

3 cups sorrel leaves, rinsed
  and shredded

⅓ cup sour cream

juice of ½ lemon

salt and freshly ground pepper

In a large pan sauté the leeks gently in the oil, stirring, until softened.
Add potato and stock and simmer, covered, for about 15 minutes, or until
potato is tender. Stir in peas and simmer, still uncovered, for an additional
5-10 minutes, or until peas are cooked. Remove from heat.

Blend contents of the saucepan with the raw sorrel leaves until smooth or
to desired texture. Stir in the cream, then chill for at least 2 hours (up to
24 hours).

Just before serving, stir in lemon juice, salt and pepper to taste.

SERVES 4

Spicy Prawn and Cucumber Soup

1 large cucumber, peeled,
    deseeded and chopped

salt

1½ cups tomato juice

1½ cups vegetable stock

2 cups yogurt

½ teaspoon ground cumin

½ teaspoon ground coriander

2 cloves garlic, crushed

2 tablespoons finely chopped
    spring onions

1 tablespoon finely chopped
    fresh mint

1 small red chili, deseeded
    and finely chopped

salt and freshly ground
    black pepper

12 freshly cooked prawns,
    peeled and deveined

extra chopped fresh mint

Place cucumber in a sieve and lightly sprinkle with salt. Set aside. Combine tomato juice, stock, yogurt, cumin, coriander, garlic, onions, mint and chili. Season to taste.

Rinse salt from cucumber and pat pieces dry with kitchen towel. Stir into soup mixture, then stir in prawns.

Chill until ready to serve, then ladle into bowls and garnish with mint.

SERVES 4 – 6

Andalusian Soup with Harissa

1 loaf dense white bread, crusts removed

2 pounds very ripe tomatoes, peeled
   and deseeded

1 teaspoon harissa (see page 22)

2 large eggs, beaten

freshly ground black pepper

7 ounces olive oil

5–6 tablespoons dry sherry

2 tablespoons finely shredded
   pancetta or prosciutto

1 cup garlic croutons (see page 4)

Tear bread into chunks and soak in 3–4 cups cold water for several minutes. Squeeze excess water from bread and place in a food processor with tomatoes, harissa, eggs and pepper. Blend together for 1–2 minutes, then slowly pour in oil until soup has a thick, mayonnaise-like consistency. Add sherry, and season to taste. Chill before serving.

Serve garnished with the shredded pancetta or prosciutto and garlic croutons.

SERVES 4–6

Sweet Potato Vichyssoise

1 tablespoon butter

2 leeks, sliced

2 large onions, roughly chopped

3 cups chicken stock

1 cup white wine

3 sweet potatoes, peeled
and finely sliced

juice and zest of 1 lime

4 ounces crème fraîche or cream

salt and freshly ground
black pepper

4 tablespoons finely chopped
fresh chives

In a saucepan melt butter and add leeks and onions. Cook over gentle heat until soft. Add stock, wine and sweet potatoes, slowly bring to a boil and simmer, covered, for 15–20 minutes until vegetables are tender. Remove from heat and cool a little.

Blend contents of pan until smooth. Stir in lime juice and zest, and crème fraîche. Season to taste. Chill until ready to serve.

Ladle into bowls and sprinkle with chopped chives.

SERVES 4

Tuscan Tomato and Basil Soup

3 tablespoons extra-virgin
   olive oil
1 large leek, thinly sliced
2 cloves garlic, finely chopped
8 large ripe tomatoes, peeled,
   deseeded and cut into chunks
4 thick slices Italian-style bread,
   crusts removed

½ teaspoon salt
freshly ground black pepper
pinch of sugar
20 fresh basil leaves,
   torn into pieces

In a saucepan heat 2 tablespoons of the oil and stir in the leek and garlic. Cook until soft. Add tomatoes and cook an additional 15-20 minutes until soft and pulpy.

Tear bread into chunks and add to saucepan. Stir, breaking up bread as the liquid is absorbed. Season with salt, pepper and a little sugar. Cool to room temperature.

To serve, stir in basil leaves and ladle into bowls. Drizzle remaining olive oil over soup and season with extra black pepper.

SERVES 4–6

Avocado Soup with Tomato Salsa

3 large ripe avocados, peeled
   and seeded

2 tablespoons fresh lime juice

1 clove garlic, crushed

3 spring onions, finely chopped

1 teaspoon ground cumin

1 cup vegetable or chicken stock

salt and freshly ground
   black pepper

1 cup yogurt

2 firm ripe tomatoes, deseeded

1 seedless cucumber, deseeded

1 spring onion, finely chopped

1 tablespoon fresh lime juice

½ teaspoon sweet chili sauce

2 tablespoons finely chopped
   fresh cilantro

Roughly chop avocado, reserving ¼ cup for the salsa. Place in a food processor with lime juice, garlic, spring onions, cumin and stock, and purée until smooth. Season with salt and pepper. Add yogurt and blend for 30 seconds, then chill soup until ready to serve.

To make tomato salsa, finely dice tomatoes and cucumber, then combine with reserved avocado. Stir in spring onion, lime juice, sweet chili sauce and chopped cilantro.

To serve, ladle soup into bowls and spoon a little tomato salsa over.

SERVES 4–6

Leek and Almond Soup

4 ounces blanched almonds

2 tablespoons olive oil

4 large leeks, thinly sliced

1 carrot, peeled and thinly sliced

4 cups chicken stock

salt and freshly ground black pepper

1 tablespoon lightly browned
   almond slices

Place blanched almonds in a food processor and blend to a coarse meal. In a saucepan heat oil and add leeks and carrot. Cook over low heat for about 5–8 minutes until soft. Add stock and slowly bring to a boil. Simmer for 15–20 minutes or until vegetables are tender. Remove from heat and cool a little.

Blend contents of pan until smooth. Return to the saucepan, stir in almond meal and heat through. Remove from heat and season to taste, then chill until required.

Serve garnished with the almond slices.

SERVES 4–6

Curried Zucchini Soup

1 tablespoon vegetable oil
1 onion, finely chopped
1 clove garlic, crushed
1 teaspoon grated fresh ginger
2 teaspoons curry powder
½ teaspoon ground coriander

½ teaspoon ground cumin
1 pound zucchini, roughly
  chopped
2 cups chicken stock
5 ounces buttermilk
sprigs of fresh cilantro
yogurt

Heat oil in a large saucepan, add onion, garlic, ginger, curry powder, coriander and cumin and cook over gentle heat for 3–4 minutes. Add zucchini and cook for 5 minutes, covered, until zucchini begins to soften. Pour in stock, and simmer for another 10 minutes or so, until zucchini are cooked. Remove from heat and cool a little.

Blend contents of pan until smooth. Chill. When cold, stir in buttermilk. Keep cool until ready to serve. Ladle into bowls and garnish with cilantro sprigs and a dollop of yogurt.

SERVES 4–6

Roasted Beet and Yogurt Soup

4 medium beets

1 tablespoon butter

1 large onion, finely chopped

2 carrots, peeled and finely
   chopped

3 cups chicken stock

2 teaspoons sugar

juice of 1 lemon

salt and freshly ground
   black pepper

1 cup creamy yogurt

1 tablespoon chopped fresh dill

extra yogurt, to serve

Preheat oven to 350°F. Wrap beets in foil and bake for 45 minutes
or until tender. Remove, set aside, then peel and finely chop when cool
enough to handle.

Meanwhile, in a saucepan melt butter and cook onion and carrots over
low heat until soft. Add prepared beets, stock and sugar, and slowly bring
to a boil. Simmer for 20–30 minutes.

Remove pan from heat and cool soup a little before blending until smooth.
Stir in lemon juice, season to taste and then stir in yogurt.

Chill until ready to serve. Ladle into bowls and garnish with dill and a swirl
of extra yogurt.

SERVES 4–6

Creamy Watercress Soup

2 bunches watercress

1 red onion, chopped

1 tablespoon oil

1 medium-sized potato,
    peeled and chopped

4 cups chicken stock

salt and freshly ground pepper

½ cup cream or mascarpone

Pick over watercress and separate leaves from stems. Set aside a few leaves for garnish.

In a large saucepan, cook onion in the oil over low heat until soft. Add the potato and cook for 2–3 minutes. Pour in the stock and bring to boil, then add the watercress leaves and simmer for 5–10 minutes. Remove from heat.

Blend contents of pan until smooth. Chill until ready to serve.

Just before serving, stir in the cream or mascarpone. Ladle into bowls and garnish with the reserved watercress leaves.

SERVES 4–6

Papaya and Pineapple Soup

2 red papayas, peeled and
   finely chopped

2 small pineapples, peeled,
   cored and finely chopped

4 tablespoons fresh lime juice

2 tablespoons tequila (optional)

1 tablespoon sugar

1 small firm yellow papaya, peeled
   and seeded (reserve few
   seeds for garnish)

2 tablespoons chopped
   fresh mint

extra fresh mint leaves

In a blender, process red papaya, half the chopped pineapple, and the lime juice, tequila (if used) and sugar. Chill until ready to serve.

Chop papaya flesh into small pieces and mix with remaining pineapple and mint.

When ready to serve, ladle fruit purée into bowls and stir in the chopped fruit. Garnish with a few papaya seeds and whole mint leaves.

SERVES 4–6

Cucumber Vichyssoise

1 tablespoon butter

2 leeks (white and pale-green
parts only), sliced

2 cups chicken or vegetable stock

½ cup white wine

2 medium-sized potatoes,
peeled and diced

½ cup cream

1 large cucumber, peeled,
deseeded and chopped

1 cup chopped fresh chives

salt and pepper

Melt butter in a saucepan, add leeks and sauté until soft but not colored
(about 5 minutes). Add stock, wine and potatoes, and simmer for 10–15
minutes, until tender.

Transfer potatoes and leeks to a blender with half the cooking liquid, and
blend to a coarse purée. Transfer to large bowl and stir in the cream.

Combine cucumber, two-thirds of the chives and the remaining cooking
liquid in blender, and purée until smooth. Combine the two purées, and
season with salt and pepper. Chill for several hours.

To serve, ladle soup into bowls and garnish with the remaining chopped
chives.

SERVES 4–6

Chilled Spanish Tomato Soup with Balsamic Vinegar

2 pounds very ripe tomatoes, chopped roughly

2 cloves garlic, chopped

¼ cup balsamic vinegar

1 teaspoon salt

2–3 saffron threads

¾ cup extra-virgin olive oil

4 hard-boiled eggs, chopped, to garnish (optional)

½ cup finely sliced Spanish ham (or use prosciutto), for garnish

crusty bread, to serve

Place tomatoes, garlic, vinegar, salt and saffron in a blender or food processor and process until smooth. Now add the oil, bit by bit, until completely incorporated. Chill soup until needed.

To serve, ladle into bowls and garnish with the egg and ham. Offer crusty bread on the side.

SERVES 6

Soup of Summer Fruits

2 pounds ripe summer fruit (e.g. plums,
   pears, cherries, berries)

2–3 cups water

2 tablespoons lemon juice

1 stick cinnamon

sugar to taste

2 tablespoons white wine

½ cup orange juice

sour cream, to serve

1 tablespoon grated lemon zest,
   for garnish

Put the fruit in a saucepan with the water, lemon juice and cinnamon stick, and simmer until fruit is tender. Strain fruit through a sieve to catch the stones or seeds and cinnamon stick, then puree flesh in a blender with the cooking liquid. Sweeten to taste, and stir in the wine and orange juice. Refrigerate until ready to serve.

Serve topped with sour cream and a sprinkle of lemon zest.

SERVES 4

Mint Soup with Pineapple

2 tablespoons butter

2 tablespoons all-purpose flour

5 cups chicken stock

1½ cups roughly chopped
   fresh mint

salt and freshly ground
   black pepper

3 ounces cream

½ cup finely chopped fresh
   pineapple

extra 2 tablespoons finely
   chopped fresh mint

½ teaspoon white sugar

In a saucepan melt butter and stir in flour. Cook, stirring, over gentle heat
until lightly browned. Slowly pour in stock, stirring continuously. Bring to a
boil and simmer for 20 minutes. Add chopped mint and cook for an
additional 5 minutes. Remove from heat and cool a little.

Blend soup until smooth. Season to taste, and stir in cream.

Refrigerate until ready to serve. Meanwhile, combine pineapple, extra mint
and sugar in a bowl. Ladle soup into bowls and garnish with a spoonful of
the minted pineapple.

SERVES 4–6

Thirty-Minute Soups

Soups, especially if you make your own stock, can seem like a slow food and this doesn't suit most people's busy lifestyles today. But in fact, thanks to the high-quality stocks and canned vegetables you can find in delis and supermarkets, soups are a great one-pot meal which can be made in less than half an hour when you get home from work.

The recipes here include great soups from all over the world – the Mediterranean, the Middle East, and east and southeast Asia.

A well-stocked refrigerator and pantry (see pages 2–3) is a great start for speedy soup-making.

Tomato and Fennel Soup with Gremolata

SOUP

2 tablespoons olive oil

2 cups finely choped fennel bulb (reserve the leaves)

14 ounces canned tomatoes, drained, juice reserved

3 cups chicken stock

¼ cup fresh lemon juice

GREMOLATA

½ cup chopped fresh parsley

2 tablespoons chopped fresh fennel leaves

2 cloves garlic, finely chopped

grated zest of ½ lemon

salt and pepper

To make soup, heat oil in a large pot, add chopped fennel and sauté gently until tender but not brown (about 5 minutes). Add tomatoes and sauté for an additional 5 minutes. Add reserved tomato juice, the stock and lemon juice, cover pot and simmer for 15 minutes.

Blend soup until smooth, then return to pot. Season to taste with salt and pepper.

To make the gremolata, simply combine all the ingredients in a bowl.

To serve, reheat soup and then ladle into bowls. Stir in a spoonful of gremolata.

SERVES 4

Eggplant and Chickpea Soup

2 tablespoons olive oil

1 large onion, finely chopped

2 small eggplants, cubed

2 large tomatoes, roughly
  chopped

¼ teaspoon ground cinnamon

¼ teaspoon ground allspice

1 tablespoon ground paprika

4 cups chicken or vegetable stock

1 cup cooked or canned
  chickpeas

salt and freshly ground
  black pepper

¼ cup creamy yogurt

1 tablespoon chopped fresh mint

In a saucepan heat oil and add onion. Cook over gentle heat until soft. Add eggplant, tomatoes and spices and cook, stirring occasionally, for 8–10 minutes. Pour in stock and bring to a boil. Simmer, covered, for about 10 minutes until eggplant is tender.

Stir in chickpeas and cook for 3–4 minutes until heated through. Season to taste. Ladle into soup bowls and garnish with spoonfuls of yogurt and mint.

Using small eggplants saves you having to salt them before cooking.

SERVES 4–6

Quick Chicken and Coconut Soup

3 cups chicken stock

1 cup coconut milk

2 teaspoons lemon zest

1 chicken breast, thinly sliced

1 stick lemongrass, finely
   chopped

4 spring onions, finely chopped

1–2 fresh or dried red chilies,
   deseeded and thinly sliced

3 tablespoons fresh lemon juice

2 tablespoons fish sauce

2 tablespoons coconut cream

1 tablespoon finely chopped
   fresh cilantro

In a saucepan slowly bring stock and coconut milk to a boil. Add lemon zest and chicken, then simmer for 8–10 minutes until chicken is tender.

Add lemongrass, spring onions, sliced chilies, lemon juice, and fish sauce. Simmer for 1–2 minutes. Ladle into bowls, distributing the chicken evenly, and garnish with a dollop of coconut cream and some chopped cilantro.

SERVES 4

Sweet Potato and Chickpea Soup

2 tablespoons olive oil

2 large carrots, peeled and finely
chopped

1 large onion, finely chopped

1 teaspoon ground cumin

4 cloves garlic, crushed

1⅓ pounds sweet potato, peeled
and finely chopped

3 cups vegetable stock

1 cup cooked (or canned)
chickpeas

salt and freshly ground
black pepper

1½ teaspoons harissa
(see page 22)

4 tablespoons creamy yogurt

extra harissa, to serve

In a large saucepan heat oil and add carrots, onion, cumin and garlic.
Cook over low heat until mixture begins to soften (about 5 minutes). Add
sweet potato and stock and bring to a boil. Simmer, covered, for 10–15
minutes until vegetables are tender. Remove from heat and cool a little.

Blend half of the soup until smooth, then return to the saucepan. Add
chickpeas and season with salt and pepper. Simmer for 5–10 minutes,
then stir in the harissa. Ladle into bowls and garnish with a swirl of
yogurt and extra harissa.

SERVES 4–6

Ocean Trout and Lemongrass Soup

4 cups fish stock

1 large tomato, chopped

2 sticks lemongrass, sliced
  into thin rounds

1 tablespoon thinly sliced
  fresh ginger

1 star anise

4 ounces rice vermicelli

4 spring onions, thinly sliced

4 ounces cherry tomatoes,
  thinly sliced

½ pound ocean trout fillet
  (skin removed), cut into
  small chunks

1 tablespoon fresh lime juice

2 teaspoons brown sugar

⅓ cup torn basil leaves

In a large saucepan place stock, tomato, lemongrass, ginger and star anise, and slowly bring to a boil. Simmer for 5 minutes to infuse flavors, then strain and pour liquid back into the saucepan.

Add vermicelli, spring onions, cherry tomatoes and ocean trout, and poach for 3–5 minutes until fish is just cooked. Add lime juice and sugar. Ladle into bowls and garnish with basil.

SERVES 4–6

Tunisian Chickpea Soup

1 quart chicken stock

1½ cups canned chickpeas,
   drained

2 teaspoons harissa

2 teaspoons ground cumin

1 teaspoon salt

2 slices sourdough or
   unleavened bread, broken
   into pieces

⅓ cup chopped fresh parsley

⅓ cup chopped fresh cilantro
   leaves

1 tablespoon chopped capers

4 soft-boiled eggs (optional)

olive oil

Simmer stock, chickpeas, harissa, cumin and salt for 15 minutes. Check seasoning.

Divide bread, herbs and capers among heated soup bowls. If desired, scoop an egg from its shell into each bowl, then ladle soup over and drizzle with olive oil.

SERVES 4

Mussel Soup with Coriander and Lemon

1 tablespoon olive oil

1 onion, finely chopped

3 cloves garlic, finely chopped

1 teaspoon ground cumin

1 teaspoon ground coriander

2 cups fish stock

1 cup white wine

¾ pound ripe tomatoes, coarsely chopped

2 pounds black mussels, scrubbed and debearded

2 tablespoons finely chopped fresh cilantro

1 tablespoon finely chopped fresh garlic chives

2 teaspoons finely grated lemon zest

In a large saucepan heat oil and add onion, garlic, cumin and coriander. Cook over gentle heat until onion is soft. Pour in stock and wine, add tomato and slowly bring to a boil. Simmer for 10 minutes.

Add mussels to the pan. Cover and cook for 5–6 minutes until mussels have opened. (Discard any that do not open.) Combine herbs and lemon zest. Ladle soup into bowls and sprinkle mixed herbs over.

SERVES 4–6

Spinach and Cabbage Minestrone

2 stalks celery, finely chopped

1 large onion, finely chopped

2 leeks, cut into thin slices

½ cup dry white wine

6 cups chicken stock

¼ green cabbage, shredded

4 zucchini, thinly sliced

½ cup dried soup pasta

salt and freshly ground
    black pepper

1 bunch spinach, washed, stems
    removed and leaves shredded

½ cup chopped fresh basil

½ cup freshly grated
    Parmesan cheese

In a saucepan simmer celery, onion and leeks with the wine over a low heat, covered, for about 10 minutes until tender. Stir from time to time. Add stock and bring to a boil. Add cabbage, zucchini and pasta and simmer for about 10 minutes until pasta is tender.

Season to taste and stir in spinach and basil. Cook for 2–3 minutes.

Ladle into soup bowls and sprinkle Parmesan cheese over.

SERVES 4–6

Prawn and Cannellini Bean Soup

14 ounces canned cannellini
   beans (white Italian kidney),
   drained

2 stalks celery, coarsely chopped

1 onion, finely chopped

1 carrot, peeled and coarsely
   chopped

3 cloves garlic, crushed

4 cups vegetable stock

2 bay leaves

1 cup tomato purée

salt and freshly ground
   black pepper

12 prawns, peeled
   and deveined

1 tablespoon finely chopped
   flat-leaf parsley

Place cannellini beans in a saucepan with celery, onion, carrot, garlic, stock and bay leaves. Bring to a boil and simmer gently for 10 minutes until flavors infuse. Remove from heat and cool a little. Discard bay leaves.

Ladle half the beans and vegetables into a food processor or blender, add tomato purée and blend until smooth.

Return soup to the pan and gently reheat. Season to taste. Add prawns and poach for 5–6 minutes until prawns are just cooked.

Ladle soup into bowls and garnish with parsley.

SERVES 4–6

Orzo and Green Pea Soup

1 tablespoon butter

1 carrot, peeled and finely chopped

1 onion, finely chopped

2 cloves garlic, finely chopped

4 cups chicken stock

1 cup orzo pasta

¼ pound fresh or frozen peas

¼ pound snow peas, trimmed and sliced

salt and freshly ground black pepper

freshly shaved Parmesan cheese

In a saucepan heat butter and add carrot, onion and garlic. Cook over gentle heat until soft. Pour in stock, bring to a boil and simmer for 4–5 minutes. Add pasta, cook for about 10 minutes until pasta is just tender.

Add peas and snow peas and cook a few minutes more, until tender. Season to taste. Ladle soup into bowls and garnish with Parmesan cheese.

SERVES 4–6

Chunky Carrot and Hazelnut Soup

2 tablespoons olive oil
  or hazelnut oil

1 onion, finely chopped

4 carrots, peeled and cubed

2 teaspoons mild curry paste

4 cups chicken or vegetable stock

4 ounces oven-roasted hazelnuts,
  roughly chopped

½ cup crème fraîche

salt and freshly ground
  black pepper

freshly chopped chives

In a saucepan heat oil and add onion, carrots and curry paste. Cover and cook over gentle heat for 10–15 minutes until carrot is tender, stirring from time to time.

Pour in stock and bring to a boil. Simmer gently for 3–4 minutes, then stir in hazelnuts and crème fraîche. Season to taste. Ladle soup into bowls and garnish with chives.

SERVES 4–6

Potato, Pumpkin and Sweet Corn Chowder

1½ tablespoons butter

2 onions, finely chopped

1 pound pumpkin, peeled and cut into small chunks

1 pound potatoes, peeled and cut into small chunks

4 cups chicken stock

16 ounces canned creamed corn

½ tablespoon Worcestershire sauce

½ cup milk

2 tablespoons finely chopped fresh chives

¼ cup crème fraîche or sour cream

In a saucepan melt butter and add onions. Cook over gentle heat until soft. Add pumpkin, potatoes and stock, and slowly bring to a boil. Simmer for 10–15 minutes until vegetables are just tender.

Add corn, Worcestershire sauce and milk. Heat through for 5–10 minutes and then stir in chives.

Ladle into soup bowls and garnish with a little crème fraîche.

SERVES 4–6

Spicy Bacon and Corn Soup

1 tablespoon olive oil

1 large red onion, finely
  chopped

1 clove garlic, finely chopped

4 ounces bacon, finely chopped

1 small red chili, deseeded
  and finely chopped

16 ounces canned tomatoes,
  roughly chopped

3 cups chicken stock

kernels from 3 corn cobs

½ cup chopped fresh
  cilantro leaves

4 tablespoons fresh lime juice

In a saucepan heat oil and add onion, garlic and bacon. Cook over medium heat until onion is soft and bacon lightly browned. Add chili and tomatoes and cook for 2–3 minutes, then pour in stock and slowly bring to a boil.

Add corn and cook for 6–8 minutes until tender. Stir in cilantro. Ladle soup into bowls and stir in a little lime juice to serve.

SERVES 4

Rustic White Bean Soup with Thyme

2 tablespoons olive oil

4 slices bacon, chopped (optional)

1 onion, chopped

1 leek, sliced

3 cloves garlic, chopped

2 stalks celery, chopped

4 sprigs fresh thyme

1 bay leaf

1½ quarts chicken stock

1 tablespoon wine vinegar

28 ounces canned cannelloni (white Italian kidney) beans, drained

salt and freshly ground black pepper

freshly shaved Parmesan, and chopped fresh thyme, to serve

corn bread, toasted

Heat the oil in a large saucepan. Add the bacon (if used) and fry for a few minutes, until crisp, then add the onion, leek, garlic, celery, thyme and bay leaf. Sauté for 10–15 minutes, until vegetables are soft and golden.

Add the stock and vinegar, and half the beans, bring to a boil and then simmer gently for about 15 minutes.

Remove the thyme and bay leaf, and purée the soup in batches until smooth. Return to the saucepan and heat through. Serve garnished with shaved Parmesan, and toasted chunks of corn bread on the side.

SERVES 4–6

Hot and Sour Tofu Soup

6 dried shiitake mushrooms, soaked in hot water for 5 minutes

5 cups chicken or vegetable stock

6 spring onions, sliced

½ cup canned bamboo shoots, drained and thinly sliced

2 teaspoons grated fresh ginger

3 tablespoons red wine vinegar

1 small red chili, deseeded and thinly sliced

3 tablespoons corn flour (finely ground cornmeal), mixed with 3 tablespoons water

1 large egg plus 1 extra egg white

7 ounces firm tofu, cut into chunks

1 bunch baby bok choy, leaves trimmed and sliced

3 tablespoons sweet soy sauce (kecap manis)

1 teaspoon sesame oil

2 tablespoons finely chopped fresh garlic chives

Drain mushrooms and thinly slice. Heat stock in a large saucepan and add mushrooms, spring onions, bamboo shoots and ginger. Slowly bring to a boil and simmer, covered, for 10 minutes.

Add vinegar and chili to the pan, then stir in cornflour mixture. Mix egg and egg white together and slowly stir into soup, beating gently after each addition. Add tofu, bok choy, sweet soy sauce and sesame oil. Cook for 2 minutes, then ladle soup into bowls and garnish with garlic chives.

SERVES 4–6

Pumpkin and Orange Soup

1 tablespoon oil

1 large onion, finely chopped

1 pound butternut squash
   (also known as butternut pumpkin)

4 cups chicken stock

zest and juice of 1 orange

salt and freshly ground black pepper

2 tablespoons finely chopped
   fresh parsley

Heat oil in a large saucepan over low heat and add onion and pumpkin. Cook for 2–3 minutes, then add stock and orange zest. Bring to a boil and simmer, covered, for 10–15 minutes until pumpkin is tender. Remove from heat and cool a little.

Blend contents of pan until smooth. Add orange juice and season to taste. Return to the pan and gently reheat. Ladle into bowls and garnish with chopped parsley.

SERVES 4–6

Potato Soup with Nettles

1 pound potatoes, peeled
  and chopped

½ pound young stinging nettles

2 tablespoons butter

1 quart chicken or vegetable
  stock

sea salt and black pepper

1 teaspoon fresh thyme leaves

1 teaspoon fresh marjoram
  leaves

⅓ cup chopped fresh chives

4 hard-boiled egg yolks,
  finely chopped

4 tablespoons sour cream

Cook the potatoes in salted water for 10 minutes, until tender, then drain. Wash and coarsely chop the nettles (wear gloves!).

Melt the butter in a saucepan, add the nettles and sauté gently for a few minutes. Add the potatoes, stock, salt, pepper, and herbs. Bring to a boil and simmer for 10 minutes or until tender.

Cool mixture slightly, then blend. Serve garnished with chopped egg yolks and the sour cream.

Nettles are at their best, for cooking, in spring. You can substitute other fresh greens, but nettles are delicious and full of vitamins and minerals.

SERVES 4–6

Garlicky Pea Soup with Thyme

1 quart chicken or vegetable stock

pinch of salt

3 tablespoons fresh thyme leaves

8 cloves garlic, peeled and
  left whole

1 pound shelled fresh peas

1-2 tablespoons of butter

freshly ground black pepper

Bring stock, salt and thyme to a simmer in a large pan. Add the garlic and simmer for about 10 minutes, to soften. Add the peas to the pan, then simmer gently for an additional 10 minutes, until garlic and peas are tender.

Remove soup from heat and blend until smooth. Return soup to the pan, stir in the butter, and season generously with freshly ground pepper. Reheat for a few minutes, then serve at once.

SERVES 4

Leek, Potato and Bacon Soup

2 tablespoons olive oil

2 leeks, thinly sliced

3 stalks celery, thinly sliced

1¾ pounds potatoes, peeled and
thinly sliced

salt and freshly ground
black pepper

4 cups chicken or vegetable stock

¼ cup crème fraîche

4 slices lean bacon, roughly
chopped

1 tablespoon finely chopped
fresh chives

In a saucepan heat oil and add leeks and celery. Cook over gentle heat until soft. Add potato and seasoning, pour in stock, then slowly bring to a boil and simmer, covered, for 15 minutes or until vegetables are tender. Remove from heat and cool a little.

Blend contents of the pan until smooth. Return to the saucepan and gently reheat. Stir in crème fraîche.

Before serving, lightly fry or grill the bacon until crisp. Ladle soup into bowls and top with the bacon and chopped chives.

SERVES 4–6

Broccoli Soup with Ricotta

2 tablespoons vegetable oil

1 large onion, thinly sliced

1 clove garlic, finely chopped

1 carrot, thinly sliced

1 stalk celery, finely chopped

4 cups chicken or vegetable stock

1⅓ pounds broccoli, trimmed
   into small florets

pinch of ground cayenne pepper

salt

½ cup ricotta cheese

In a saucepan heat oil and add onion, garlic, carrot and celery. Cook over gentle heat until soft. Pour in stock and bring to a boil. Add broccoli and cook until tender. Remove from heat and cool a little.

Blend contents of the saucepan until smooth, then gently reheat. Season to taste with cayenne pepper and salt. Ladle into bowls and spoon in a couple of dollops of ricotta.

SERVES 4

Italian Chickpea and Pasta Soup

2 tablespoons olive oil

1 onion, finely chopped

2 cloves garlic, finely chopped

½ teaspoon dried thyme

1 cup canned tomatoes, drained and chopped

3 cups vegetable stock

1 cup canned chickpeas, drained

½ cup rice pasta (as orzo) or soup pasta (as ditalini)

salt and freshly ground black pepper

½ cup chopped fresh parsley

½ cup freshly grated Parmesan cheese

In a saucepan heat oil and add onion, garlic and thyme. Cook over gentle heat until onion is soft. Add tomatoes and cook for 4–5 minutes until mixture has thickened and reduced a little. Stir in stock and chickpeas. Bring to a boil and simmer for 5–10 minutes. Remove from heat, and cool.

Blend half the soup until smooth, return to saucepan and gently reheat. Stir in pasta and cook for 5 minutes until tender. Season to taste. Stir in parsley and ladle soup into bowls. Garnish with a sprinkling of Parmesan cheese.

SERVES 4

Avocado Soup with Prawns

1 red onion, diced

2 stalks celery, finely chopped

4 cups chicken stock

1 bay leaf

4 sprigs fresh parsley

salt and freshly ground
    black pepper

2 large avocadoes, peeled and
    seeded, flesh chopped roughly

1 cup cooked, shelled and
    deveined prawns

1 cup sour cream

3 tablespoons chopped chives

Place onion, celery, stock, bay leaf, parsley, salt and pepper in a large
saucepan and bring to a boil. Simmer for 15 minutes and then strain,
reserving stock.

Place avocadoes in a blender or food processor and puree while slowly
adding stock. When mixture is smooth, return to saucepan and
heat gently. Add prawns and continue to cook very gently until prawns
are heated through (do not boil).

Serve in warmed bowls, garnished with a dollop of sour cream and
a sprinkling of chopped chives.

SERVES 4–6

Index

PENGUIN BOOKS

Published by the Penguin Group
Penguin Group (Australia)
250 Camberwell Road, Camberwell, Victoria 3124, Australia
(a division of Pearson Australia Group Pty Ltd)
Penguin Group (USA) Inc.
375 Hudson Street, New York, New York 10014, USA
Penguin Group (Canada)
90 Eglinton Avenue East, Suite 700, Toronto ON M4P 2Y3, Canada
(a division of Pearson Penguin Canada Inc.)
Penguin Books Ltd
80 Strand, London WC2R 0RL, England
Penguin Ireland
25 St Stephen's Green, Dublin 2, Ireland
(a division of Penguin Books Ltd)
Penguin Books India Pvt Ltd
11 Community Centre, Panchsheel Park, New Delhi – 110 017, India
Penguin Group (NZ)
67 Apollo Drive, Mairangi Bay, Auckland 1310, New Zealand
(a division of Pearson New Zealand Ltd)
Penguin Books (South Africa) (Pty) Ltd
24 Sturdee Avenue, Rosebank, Johannesburg 2196, South Africa

Penguin Books Ltd, Registered Offices: 80 Strand, London, WC2R 0RL, England

First published by Penguin Group (Australia), 2007

10 9 8 7 6 5 4 3 2 1

This 2010 edition published exclusively for Barnes & Noble, Inc.

ISBN: 978-1-4351-2749-4

Special Markets ISBN: 978-0-14-311782-7

Many thanks to Danielle Toigo of Creative Homewares in Albert Park, Freedom Furniture in South Yarra,
and Matchbox in Armadale, all of whom provided beautiful props.

Design by Elizabeth Theodosiadis and Claire Tice © Penguin Group (Australia)
Photography by Julie Renouf
Food styling by Virginia Walsh
Typeset by Post Pre-press Group, Brisbane, Queensland
Color reproduction by Splitting Image, Clayton, Victoria
Printed in China by South China Printing Co. Ltd